HOW DO A PROJECT MANAGER DELIVER BAD NEWS

TEAM MANAGEMENT | SUCCESSFUL PROJECTS | COMMUNICATION MANAGEMENT | STAKEHOLDERS MANAGEMENT | REPORTS

ANGELA SIRBU, MBA. PMP

© 2024 by Angela Sirbu, MBA. PMP. All rights reserved.

No part of this book may be reproduced or utilized in any form or by any means, electronic or mechanical, including photocopying, recording, or by any information storage and retrieval system, without permission in writing from the publisher.

First Edition 2024

Published by Angela Sirbu, MBA. PMP

CONTENTS

INTRODUCTION

CHAPTER 1: INTRODUCTION TO DELIVERING BAD NEWS

CHAPTER 2: PREPARING FOR THE CONVERSATION

CHAPTER 3: COMMUNICATION TECHNIQUES

CHAPTER 4: DELIVERING THE NEWS

CHAPTER 5: HANDLING DIFFERENT STAKEHOLDERS

CHAPTER 6: MAINTAINING MORALE AND MOTIVATION

CHAPTER 7: LEARNING FROM THE EXPERIENCE

CHAPTER 8: BUILDING RESILIENCE

CHAPTER 9: CASE STUDIES AND REAL-LIFE EXAMPLES

CHAPTER 10: ETHICS AND PROFESSIONALISM

CHAPTER 11: TOOLS AND RESOURCES

CHAPTER 12: THE ROLE OF FEEDBACK

CHAPTER 13: FUTURE TRENDS IN PROJECT MANAGEMENT COMMUNICATION

CHAPTER 14: CONCLUSION AND FINAL THOUGHTS

INTRODUCTION

Navigating the complexities of project management often involves more than just careful planning, resource allocation, and timeline adherence. One of the most challenging aspects is delivering bad news. Whether it's a delay in the project timeline, budget overruns, or unforeseen obstacles, how a project manager communicates these setbacks can significantly impact team morale, stakeholder trust, and the ultimate success of the project. This book delves into the nuanced art of delivering bad news in a professional and effective manner, integrating principles of team management, communication strategies, and stakeholder engagement.

Effective communication is the cornerstone of successful project management. It is crucial not only to convey progress and achievements but also to address issues and challenges transparently. This requires a set of skills that go beyond technical expertise—empathy, diplomacy, and strategic thinking become indispensable tools. The approach you take in delivering bad news can either foster a collaborative environment or create a culture of fear and mistrust. This book aims to equip you with the knowledge and techniques to handle these difficult conversations with poise and confidence.

Real-world examples, expert insights, and practical advice are combined to offer a comprehensive guide. Topics covered include understanding the psychological impact of bad news, preparing for difficult conversations, crafting the right message, and managing the aftermath. You'll learn how to tailor your communication to different stakeholders, ensuring that your message is clear, respectful, and constructive. Additionally, strategies for maintaining team cohesion and motivation during challenging times are discussed in depth.

By mastering the art of delivering bad news, you will not only enhance your leadership capabilities but also contribute to a culture of transparency and resilience within your team. This book is an essential resource for project managers who aspire to lead with integrity and effectiveness, even in the face of adversity.

Chapter 1: Introduction to Delivering Bad News

The Importance of Communication in Project Management

Effective communication stands as the backbone of successful project management. A project manager's ability to convey information clearly and accurately is paramount to the success of any project. The role of communication in project management is multifaceted, encompassing the dissemination of information, the resolution of conflicts, the establishment of relationships, and the facilitation of collaboration among team members.

At its core, communication ensures that all stakeholders are aligned with the project's goals, scope, and timelines. It serves as the medium through which expectations are set and managed. Without clear communication, team members may operate under different assumptions, leading to misunderstandings and misaligned objectives. This can result in delays, cost overruns, and even project failure. A project manager must, therefore, be adept at articulating the project's vision, objectives, and deliverables to all stakeholders, ensuring that everyone is on the same page.

Equally important is the role of communication in conflict resolution. Projects often bring together individuals with diverse backgrounds and perspectives, which can lead to disagreements and conflicts. A project manager must be skilled in navigating these conflicts through effective communication. This involves not only addressing the immediate issue but also understanding the underlying concerns of all parties involved. By fostering an open and transparent communication environment, a project manager can mediate conflicts and arrive at mutually acceptable solutions, thereby maintaining team cohesion and productivity.

Building and maintaining relationships is another critical aspect of communication in project management. Trust and rapport are essential for effective teamwork. A project manager must invest time and effort in building strong relationships with team members, stakeholders, and clients. This involves regular check-ins, active listening, and providing constructive feedback. When team members feel heard and valued, they are more likely to be engaged and motivated, which in turn enhances overall project performance.

Furthermore, communication plays a pivotal role in facilitating collaboration. Projects often require the coordination of multiple tasks and the integration of various skill sets. Effective communication ensures that team members are aware of their roles and responsibilities, as well as how their work contributes to the larger project. This fosters a sense of ownership and accountability, which is essential for the successful completion of the project. Regular meetings, status updates, and collaborative tools can help in maintaining a continuous flow of information, enabling team members to work together seamlessly.

In the realm of delivering bad news, communication becomes even more critical. A project manager must approach this task with sensitivity and transparency. Whether it is a delay in the project timeline, a budget overrun, or a change in project scope, bad news must be communicated promptly and honestly. This not only helps in managing stakeholder expectations but also in finding solutions to mitigate the impact. A project manager must be prepared to explain the reasons behind the bad news, outline the steps being taken to address the issue, and provide a clear plan for moving forward. This approach helps in maintaining trust and confidence among stakeholders, even in challenging situations.

In conclusion, communication is an indispensable tool in the arsenal of a project manager. It underpins every aspect of project management, from planning and execution to monitoring and closure. Mastering the art of communication enables a project manager to navigate the complexities of project management effectively, ensuring that projects are delivered successfully, even in the face of adversity.

Understanding the Impact of Bad News

The ripple effect of bad news in the realm of project management is profound and multifaceted. When a project manager is tasked with delivering unfavorable updates, the impact stretches far beyond the immediate recipients. It seeps into every corner of the project ecosystem, affecting team dynamics, stakeholder relationships, and the overall trajectory of the project.

Imagine a scenario where a project has hit a significant roadblock. The initial shockwave of this news is felt most acutely by the project team. These individuals, who have invested time, energy, and often personal pride into the project, may experience a range of emotions from disappointment to frustration. Morale can plummet, leading to decreased productivity and engagement. The once cohesive unit may begin to fracture as blame is assigned and trust erodes.

For stakeholders, bad news can trigger a cascade of concerns. Investors may worry about financial implications, clients might fear delays and unmet expectations, and upper management could question the project's viability. Each of these concerns can lead to increased scrutiny, pressure, and demands for accountability. The project manager, already burdened with the task of communicating the bad news, now faces the added challenge of managing heightened expectations and anxiety.

The broader organizational impact cannot be overlooked. Projects often operate within a larger strategic framework, and setbacks can have ripple effects on other initiatives. Resource allocation might need to be reconsidered, timelines adjusted, and priorities reshuffled. The interdependencies of modern project environments mean that bad news in one area can quickly spill over into others, creating a domino effect that disrupts the entire organization.

On a personal level, delivering bad news can take a toll on the project manager themselves. The responsibility of conveying difficult information can be emotionally draining. The fear of damaging relationships, losing credibility, or facing backlash can weigh heavily. This stress can affect the project manager's decision-making abilities, communication effectiveness, and overall well-being. It is not uncommon for project managers to experience a sense of isolation as they navigate these challenging waters.

However, the impact of bad news is not solely negative. It also presents an opportunity for growth, learning, and resilience.

When handled with transparency, empathy, and a focus on solutions, the delivery of bad news can strengthen relationships and build trust. Stakeholders appreciate honesty and a proactive approach to problem-solving. Teams can rally together, finding innovative ways to overcome obstacles and emerge stronger.

The key lies in understanding the multifaceted impact of bad news and preparing to address it comprehensively. Project managers must be adept at reading the room, gauging the emotional temperature, and tailoring their communication strategies accordingly. They need to provide clear, concise information while also offering support and reassurance. By acknowledging the emotional and practical implications of bad news, project managers can foster a culture of resilience and adaptability.

Bad news, while challenging, is an inevitable part of the project management landscape. Its impact is far-reaching, touching every aspect of the project and its participants. By approaching it with sensitivity and strategic foresight, project managers can navigate these turbulent waters, mitigating negative effects and steering the project back on course.

Common Scenarios Requiring Tough Conversations

Project managers often find themselves in situations where delivering bad news is unavoidable. These scenarios can range widely and may include issues such as project delays, budget overruns, resource shortages, or even the complete failure of a project. Each of these scenarios requires a different approach, yet they all demand honesty, transparency, and sensitivity.

One common scenario is a project delay. Despite the best planning and efforts, unforeseen circumstances such as technical difficulties, supplier delays, or unexpected regulatory changes can push timelines beyond their original deadlines. Communicating this to stakeholders, especially those with high expectations, can be daunting. The key is to present the delay as soon as it becomes apparent, providing a clear explanation of the reasons behind it. Offering a revised timeline and outlining the steps being taken to mitigate the delay can also help to manage expectations and maintain trust.

Budget overruns are another frequent challenge. Projects often encounter unexpected costs due to scope changes, inaccurate initial estimates, or unforeseen complications. When faced with this, a project manager must prepare a detailed account of the financial situation and be ready to justify each expense. It's crucial to propose a plan for addressing the overrun, whether it involves cutting costs elsewhere, requesting additional funds, or finding alternative solutions. Transparency in financial matters is essential to sustain stakeholder confidence and support.

Resource shortages can also lead to difficult conversations. Whether it's a shortage of manpower, materials, or technology, these shortages can significantly impact project progress. In such cases, it's important to communicate the issue promptly and outline the potential effects on the project. Proposing a reallocation of resources, seeking external support, or adjusting project scope can demonstrate proactive problem-solving. Acknowledging the challenge while focusing on potential solutions can help to reassure stakeholders.

Sometimes, the news is even more severe, such as the complete failure of a project. This could be due to insurmountable technical challenges, a shift in market conditions, or a strategic decision by the organization. Breaking this news requires a high degree of sensitivity and a well-thought-out communication strategy. The project manager should provide a comprehensive analysis of what led to the failure, what lessons have been learned, and how these lessons will be applied to future projects. Emphasizing the value of the experience gained, despite the failure, can help to soften the blow and highlight the commitment to continuous improvement.

Another scenario involves conflicts within the project team. Interpersonal issues, differing opinions, or misaligned goals can create a challenging environment. Addressing these conflicts openly and constructively is crucial. The project manager should facilitate a discussion that allows all parties to express their concerns and work towards a resolution. Highlighting common goals and encouraging collaboration can help to restore harmony and refocus the team on the project objectives.

Changes in project scope or objectives can also necessitate tough conversations. Stakeholders may have differing opinions on the direction of the project, leading to conflicts or dissatisfaction. Clear communication about the reasons for the change, its impact on the project, and how it aligns with the overall goals of the organization is vital. Engaging stakeholders in the decision-making process can also help to gain their buy-in and support.

In each of these scenarios, the project manager's role is to communicate effectively, manage expectations, and maintain trust. By approaching these tough conversations with honesty, transparency, and a focus on solutions, project managers can navigate the challenges and maintain strong relationships with their stakeholders.

The Role of a Project Manager in Crisis Situations

In the complex world of project management, crises are inevitable. A project manager's role during these turbulent times becomes pivotal, demanding a unique blend of skills, presence, and strategic thinking. The ability to steer a project through crisis situations requires not just technical prowess but also emotional intelligence and resilient leadership.

When a crisis strikes, the first and foremost task for a project manager is to maintain composure. Panic can spread quickly through a team, and a leader who remains calm and collected sets a tone of confidence and control. This calm demeanor helps in assessing the situation more clearly and making rational decisions without the cloud of anxiety.

Communication is a critical tool in a project manager's arsenal during a crisis. Transparent, timely, and accurate information must be shared with all stakeholders to manage expectations and reduce uncertainty. Crafting messages that are clear and concise, yet empathetic, is essential. The project manager must ensure that the team is aware of the situation, understands the potential impacts, and knows the steps being taken to address the issues. This openness fosters trust and collaboration, which are crucial in navigating through the storm.

A project manager must also be adept at problem-solving and decision-making under pressure. This involves quickly identifying the root cause of the crisis, evaluating possible solutions, and implementing the most effective course of action. It's important to rely on data and evidence where possible, but also to trust one's instincts and experience. Flexibility and adaptability are key, as crises often evolve and new challenges can emerge unexpectedly.

Another significant aspect of handling crises is stakeholder management. Different stakeholders will have varying concerns and priorities; thus, a project manager must tailor their communication and engagement strategies accordingly. Keeping clients, sponsors, and team members informed and involved can help to mitigate the negative impacts of the crisis and maintain their support and confidence.

Resource management becomes even more critical during crises. A project manager must reassess the allocation of resources, which may include budget, personnel, and time. This reassessment often involves making tough decisions, such as reallocating team members to more critical tasks or cutting non-essential activities to focus on crisis resolution. The ability to prioritize effectively ensures that the most pressing issues are addressed promptly.

Moreover, a project manager must act as a motivator and morale booster. Crises can be demoralizing, and team members may feel overwhelmed or disheartened. A project manager should recognize the efforts and contributions of the team, provide encouragement, and maintain a positive outlook. This support can help to sustain team cohesion and drive, even in the face of adversity.

Documenting the crisis and the responses taken is another important responsibility. This documentation serves as a valuable learning tool for future projects. By analyzing what went wrong and what strategies were effective, a project manager can help the organization build resilience and improve crisis management processes.

In essence, a project manager in crisis situations must wear many hats: a calm leader, an effective communicator, a strategic thinker, a resource manager, and a motivator. The ability to deliver bad news with honesty and empathy, while steering the project back on track, defines the true essence of project management excellence in challenging times.

Chapter 2: Preparing for the Conversation

Gathering All Necessary Information

A project manager often finds themselves in the unenviable position of delivering bad news. To do so effectively, it's crucial to gather all necessary information before communicating with stakeholders. The initial step involves understanding the full scope of the issue. This means diving deep into the project's details, timelines, and any contributing factors that have led to the current situation. Accurate data is the foundation of clear, honest communication.

Begin by reviewing all project documentation. This includes project plans, progress reports, emails, and meeting notes. These documents will provide a comprehensive view of the project's trajectory and highlight where things may have gone off course. Identifying discrepancies between planned and actual progress is essential. Look for patterns or recurring issues that might have compounded over time.

Next, engage with your team members. They are on the front lines and can offer invaluable insights into what has transpired. Schedule one-on-one meetings to discuss their perspectives and gather firsthand accounts of the project's challenges. This is also an opportunity to gauge the morale and sentiments of the team, which can be a critical factor when delivering bad news. Listening to your team's concerns and suggestions can provide a more nuanced understanding of the problem and potential solutions.

Stakeholder expectations must also be considered. Review the original project scope, objectives, and any changes that have been agreed upon. Understanding what stakeholders expect versus what is being delivered will help in framing the bad news. It's important to align your message with their priorities and concerns. This alignment will make the conversation more focused and constructive.

Once you have gathered all the information from documents, team members, and stakeholders, it's time to analyze the data. Identify the root cause of the problem. Was it a lack of resources, unforeseen technical issues, or perhaps miscommunication? Pinpointing the cause will not only help in explaining the situation but also in proposing viable solutions. It's not enough to just present the bad news; offering a path forward is equally important.

Consider the timing and setting for delivering the news. Bad news should never be delivered hastily or in an inappropriate setting. Choose a time when stakeholders are likely to be most receptive and ensure a private, distraction-free environment. This shows respect for the gravity of the situation and allows for a more focused discussion.

Prepare your message meticulously. Start with a clear, concise statement of the issue. Follow this with a detailed explanation backed by the information you have gathered. Be transparent about what went wrong and why. Honesty is crucial; sugarcoating or withholding information can lead to a loss of trust. After presenting the problem, outline the steps that will be taken to address it. This demonstrates proactive management and a commitment to finding solutions.

Anticipate questions and concerns that stakeholders might have. Prepare answers based on the data and insights you have collected. This will help in maintaining control of the conversation and providing reassurance. It's also important to be empathetic. Acknowledge the impact of the bad news on stakeholders and express a genuine commitment to making things right.

In essence, the key to delivering bad news effectively lies in thorough preparation. By gathering all necessary information, a project manager can communicate with confidence, clarity, and compassion, ultimately fostering a more resilient and cooperative project environment.

Anticipating Questions and Reactions

A project manager's role involves tackling various challenges, and delivering bad news is one of the most daunting tasks. When faced with this responsibility, it is crucial to anticipate the questions and reactions that may arise from stakeholders. By preparing for these responses, a project manager can navigate the situation more effectively and maintain trust and confidence within the team and with clients.

Understanding the concerns of stakeholders requires a deep knowledge of the project's scope, timeline, and objectives. Stakeholders will likely have immediate questions about the impact of the bad news on the project's overall success. They may inquire about how the issue will affect the schedule, budget, and quality of deliverables. Being prepared with detailed and honest answers can help mitigate their concerns and demonstrate a proactive approach to problem-solving.

Stakeholders might also express frustration or disappointment upon receiving bad news. It's important to acknowledge their emotions and provide a space for them to voice their concerns. Empathy plays a key role in these interactions. By showing understanding and validating their feelings, a project manager can build a rapport that fosters open communication and collaboration.

Another common reaction is the search for accountability. Stakeholders may want to know who is responsible for the issue and what steps are being taken to address it. A project manager should be ready to present a clear analysis of the situation, including the root cause of the problem and the measures being implemented to prevent similar issues in the future. This transparency not only addresses the immediate concern but also reassures stakeholders that lessons are being learned and improvements are being made.

In some cases, stakeholders may propose solutions or suggest changes to the project plan. A project manager should be open to these suggestions and evaluate them objectively. Engaging stakeholders in the problem-solving process can lead to innovative solutions and a sense of shared ownership of the project's success. It also demonstrates that their input is valued and that the project manager is committed to finding the best possible outcome.

Anticipating questions and reactions also involves preparing for the worst-case scenario. Stakeholders may express a lack of confidence in the project's viability or in the project manager's ability to lead. To address this, a project manager should have a contingency plan in place and be ready to discuss alternative strategies. This preparedness shows a commitment to the project's goals and a willingness to adapt to changing circumstances.

Effective communication is at the heart of delivering bad news. A project manager should use clear, concise language and avoid jargon that may confuse or alienate stakeholders. Visual aids, such as charts or diagrams, can help illustrate the situation and make complex information more accessible. Additionally, providing regular updates and maintaining open lines of communication can prevent surprises and build a foundation of trust.

Delivering bad news is never easy, but by anticipating questions and reactions, a project manager can navigate this challenging task with confidence and poise. By preparing thoroughly, showing empathy, and maintaining transparency, a project manager can turn a difficult situation into an opportunity for growth and improvement, ultimately steering the project towards a successful outcome.

Choosing the Right Time and Place

Selecting the appropriate time and place to deliver unfavorable news is a crucial aspect of a project manager's role. The environment and timing can significantly impact how the message is received and processed by the team or stakeholders. It requires a delicate balance of empathy, strategy, and situational awareness.

Consider the timing first. Delivering bad news at the end of the workday might seem like a way to avoid immediate conflict, but it can leave recipients stewing in their emotions overnight, leading to anxiety and decreased productivity. On the other hand, breaking the news first thing in the morning allows for a full day of processing and problem-solving, but it might set a negative tone for the day. Mid-morning or early afternoon often provide a sweet spot; the team has had time to settle into their day, and there are still hours left to discuss and address the issue.

Equally important is choosing the right moment within the project's lifecycle. If the bad news pertains to a significant delay or budget overrun, it is best to communicate this as soon as the information is confirmed. Delaying the announcement can lead to a loss of trust and exacerbate the problem. Conversely, if the bad news is less time-sensitive, it might be wise to wait until a regular meeting or a less stressful period in the project.

The physical setting also plays a significant role. A private, quiet space where you can have an uninterrupted conversation is ideal. This ensures confidentiality and allows for an open, honest dialogue. Avoid delivering bad news in public areas or during large meetings, as this can lead to embarrassment or a defensive reaction. A conference room or a private office provides a controlled environment where emotions can be managed more effectively.

The atmosphere should be conducive to a respectful and empathetic exchange. Arrange seating in a way that feels collaborative rather than confrontational. Sitting across a large desk can create a barrier, both physically and emotionally. Instead, opt for a round table or sit adjacent to the person, which fosters a sense of partnership and mutual respect.

In virtual settings, choosing the right platform and ensuring a stable connection are vital. Video calls are preferable to phone calls or emails, as they allow for visual cues and a more personal touch. Ensure that both parties have a quiet, private space for the conversation and that the technology is functioning well to avoid miscommunication.

Preparation is key. Anticipate the questions and concerns that might arise and have data or solutions ready to discuss. This shows that you have thought through the implications and are committed to finding a way forward. Practice delivering the message in a calm, clear, and compassionate manner, focusing on the facts and the steps to mitigate the issue.

The emotional state of the recipient should also be considered. If you know that someone is dealing with personal stress or has just received other bad news, it might be worth delaying the conversation slightly, if circumstances allow. Sensitivity to their emotional threshold can make a significant difference in how the news is received.

In essence, the effective delivery of bad news hinges on a thoughtful consideration of timing, setting, and approach. By carefully orchestrating these elements, a project manager can foster a more constructive and less traumatic experience for all involved.

Developing a Clear Message

Crafting a message that conveys unwelcome news requires precision, empathy, and clarity. The process begins with understanding the core of the message you need to deliver. One must distill the essence of the situation, stripping away any superfluous details to focus solely on the critical points. This clarity allows for a message that is not only understandable but also straightforward, minimizing the potential for confusion or misinterpretation.

The tone of the message is equally important. Maintaining a balance between professionalism and empathy can significantly influence how the message is received. A cold, detached tone can exacerbate the negative impact, while an overly emotional approach can undermine the seriousness of the situation. Striking the right balance ensures that the message is both respectful and sincere, acknowledging the feelings of the recipients while maintaining the gravity of the situation.

Choosing the appropriate medium for delivering the message is another crucial aspect. A face-to-face meeting, whether in person or via video call, often allows for a more personal touch and immediate feedback. This method provides an opportunity for the recipient to ask questions and for the project manager to offer immediate clarifications. However, there are instances where a written communication, such as an email, might be more suitable, particularly when the information needs to be documented for future reference.

The structure of the message should be carefully considered. Start with a brief introduction that outlines the purpose of the communication. This sets the stage for the main content, preparing the recipient for what is to come. Follow this with a clear, concise statement of the bad news. Avoid burying the key information in a sea of words; instead, present it up front to ensure it is immediately understood. After delivering the core message, provide a detailed explanation of the reasons behind the decision or situation. Transparency in this part of the message can help build trust and mitigate feelings of resentment or confusion.

Providing context is essential. When recipients understand the factors that led to the unfavorable outcome, they are more likely to accept and understand the situation. Detail any external constraints, internal challenges, or unforeseen circumstances that contributed to the decision. This not only clarifies the rationale but also demonstrates that the decision was not made lightly.

Anticipate the questions and concerns of the recipients. Addressing these proactively within the message can help alleviate anxiety and demonstrate that you have considered their perspectives. Offering potential solutions or next steps can also help shift the focus from the problem to the path forward. This forward-thinking approach can instill a sense of hope and direction, even in the face of bad news.

Finally, be prepared for the emotional reactions that may follow. Acknowledging the impact of the news on the recipients shows empathy and understanding. Offer your support and be willing to engage in further discussion if needed. This not only helps to manage the immediate reaction but also fosters a sense of solidarity and teamwork.

In essence, developing a clear message when delivering bad news is about more than just conveying information. It is about doing so with integrity, empathy, and a focus on maintaining strong, respectful relationships.

Chapter 3: Communication Techniques

Active Listening Skills

Active listening is an essential skill for project managers, especially when delivering bad news. It is more than just hearing words; it involves fully comprehending the message being conveyed, understanding the emotions behind it, and providing thoughtful feedback. This skill is crucial in managing difficult conversations and maintaining trust within a team.

When a project manager needs to deliver bad news, the initial reaction from team members can range from disappointment to frustration. Active listening helps in acknowledging these emotions and addressing them appropriately. By giving full attention to the speaker, a project manager can pick up on non-verbal cues such as body language and tone of voice, which often reveal more than words alone. This attentiveness demonstrates empathy and respect, making the conversation more constructive.

One of the fundamental components of active listening is maintaining eye contact. This non-verbal gesture signifies that the listener is fully engaged and values what the speaker is saying. In a project setting, when bad news is being delivered, maintaining eye contact can help to soften the blow, showing that the manager is sincere and present in the moment.

Another critical aspect is avoiding interruptions. Allowing team members to express their thoughts and feelings without cutting them off is vital. Interruptions can make individuals feel undervalued and unheard, exacerbating negative emotions. By letting them speak freely, a project manager can gain a deeper understanding of their concerns and respond more effectively.

Paraphrasing and summarizing what the speaker has said are also beneficial techniques. These methods ensure that the message has been correctly understood and provide an opportunity for clarification. For instance, a project manager might say, "It sounds like you're concerned about the project's timeline. Is that correct?" This approach not only confirms understanding but also shows that the manager is actively engaged in the conversation.

Empathy plays a significant role in active listening. Project managers should strive to put themselves in their team members' shoes, understanding their perspectives and emotions. This empathetic approach can help in building stronger relationships and fostering a supportive environment. When delivering bad news, expressing empathy can mitigate some of the negative impacts and help the team navigate through the challenges together.

Reflective listening is another technique that can be effective. This involves reflecting back the emotions that the speaker is conveying. For example, a project manager might say, "I can see that this news is really disappointing for you." Acknowledging emotions in this way can validate the speaker's feelings and create a space for open and honest dialogue.

Lastly, providing feedback is an integral part of active listening. It should be constructive and aimed at finding solutions. For instance, after delivering bad news, a project manager might ask, "What can we do to address this issue?" This question not only shows that the manager values the team's input but also shifts the focus towards problem-solving.

Incorporating active listening skills can transform the way a project manager delivers bad news. It fosters an environment of trust and respect, making it easier to navigate through difficult conversations. By truly listening, understanding, and responding with empathy, a project manager can maintain team morale and work collaboratively towards overcoming challenges.

Empathy and Emotional Intelligence

Empathy and emotional intelligence stand as pillars for any project manager tasked with delivering bad news. These qualities transform the daunting responsibility into a more humane and effective interaction. Empathy allows the project manager to step into the shoes of their audience, understanding their feelings, concerns, and perspectives. This understanding is crucial, as it enables the manager to tailor their communication in a way that acknowledges the emotional impact of the news.

Emotional intelligence, on the other hand, involves the ability to recognize and manage one's own emotions while also being attuned to the emotions of others. For a project manager, this means remaining composed and clear-headed even when faced with difficult circumstances. It involves regulating one's emotional responses to maintain a calm and supportive demeanor, which can significantly influence how the news is received.

When preparing to deliver bad news, a project manager with high emotional intelligence will anticipate the potential emotional reactions of their team or stakeholders. This foresight allows them to prepare supportive responses and strategies to address concerns and mitigate negative impacts. For instance, if the bad news involves a project delay, the manager might acknowledge the disappointment and frustration this may cause, while simultaneously offering a clear plan for moving forward.

Effective communication in these situations often begins with active listening. By giving the affected parties space to express their feelings and concerns, the project manager demonstrates empathy and validates their emotions. This can be as simple as nodding in understanding, or as involved as repeating back what has been said to show that it has been heard and comprehended. Such gestures foster an environment of trust and respect, which is essential when navigating difficult conversations.

The choice of words and tone also plays a significant role. A project manager should aim to be honest yet compassionate, delivering the news in a straightforward manner without sugarcoating it, but also without being unnecessarily harsh. This delicate balance helps to maintain credibility while also showing care and consideration for the emotional well-being of the team.

Non-verbal communication is equally important. Maintaining eye contact, using open body language, and being mindful of one's facial expressions can all convey sincerity and empathy. A manager who appears distracted or indifferent may inadvertently exacerbate the emotional distress of the recipients. Therefore, being fully present in the moment is critical.

After delivering the news, emotional intelligence continues to be important. The project manager should be prepared to offer support and guidance, helping the team to process the information and explore constructive ways to move forward. This might involve facilitating a discussion on potential solutions, offering additional resources, or simply providing a listening ear.

Incorporating empathy and emotional intelligence into the process of delivering bad news not only helps to soften the immediate blow but also strengthens the overall relationship between the project manager and their team. It builds a foundation of trust and mutual respect, which can enhance collaboration and resilience in the face of future challenges. By prioritizing these qualities, a project manager can navigate the complexities of their role with greater effectiveness and humanity.

Non-Verbal Communication

Non-verbal communication plays a pivotal role in the delicate task of delivering bad news. The subtle cues conveyed through body language, facial expressions, and tone of voice often speak louder than words themselves. A project manager must be acutely aware of these elements to ensure that the message is not only delivered but also received with the intended empathy and clarity.

The eyes, often referred to as the windows to the soul, are powerful tools in non-verbal communication. Maintaining eye contact can convey sincerity and confidence, while averting one's gaze may suggest discomfort or dishonesty. A project manager, when delivering unfavorable news, should strive to maintain a steady yet gentle gaze, signaling to the recipient that they are fully engaged and empathetic to the situation. However, it is crucial to balance this with sensitivity, as prolonged or intense eye contact can be perceived as confrontational.

Facial expressions are another critical component. A furrowed brow, a tight-lipped smile, or a grimace can all convey various emotions that words might fail to express. A project manager should aim for a neutral yet compassionate expression. A slight nod or a softening of the eyes can help in demonstrating understanding and concern. These subtle gestures can make a significant difference in how the message is perceived and can help in mitigating the emotional impact of the news.

Body posture is equally significant. An open and relaxed stance can make the recipient feel more at ease, whereas crossed arms or a rigid posture can create a barrier and imply defensiveness. Leaning slightly forward can indicate attentiveness and a willingness to engage in a constructive dialogue. It is essential for a project manager to be mindful of their posture, ensuring it aligns with the supportive and empathetic tone they wish to convey.

The tone of voice is an often-underestimated aspect of non-verbal communication. The way words are spoken can influence their meaning and the emotional response they elicit. A calm, steady, and warm tone can help in cushioning the impact of bad news, whereas a hurried or harsh tone can exacerbate the recipient's distress. Pausing appropriately and speaking at a measured pace allows the recipient to process the information and signals that the project manager is not rushing through the conversation.

Gestures, such as the use of hands, can also enhance or detract from the message. Gentle hand movements can complement verbal communication and help in emphasizing key points. Conversely, exaggerated or abrupt gestures can distract or even alarm the recipient. It is beneficial for a project manager to use controlled and deliberate gestures that align with the message's tone.

The setting in which the conversation takes place can further influence non-verbal communication. A private and comfortable environment can help in fostering a sense of security and openness. The choice of space should minimize distractions and interruptions, allowing both parties to focus on the conversation at hand.

In essence, non-verbal communication requires a project manager to be observant and adaptive. By paying close attention to their own non-verbal cues and those of the recipient, they can navigate the challenging task of delivering bad news with greater sensitivity and effectiveness. The subtle interplay of eye contact, facial expressions, posture, tone of voice, and gestures can collectively convey empathy and support, softening the blow of unfavorable news and paving the way for a more constructive and understanding dialogue.

Framing the Message Positively

When confronted with the necessity of delivering bad news, the manner in which the message is framed can significantly influence how it is received. The act of conveying unwelcome information doesn't have to be a purely negative experience. By adopting a positive framing technique, a project manager can soften the impact and potentially turn a challenging situation into an opportunity for growth and improvement.

Consider the language and tone used when presenting the news. Instead of focusing solely on the negative aspects, emphasize any positive elements or potential benefits that may arise. For instance, if a project deadline is being pushed back, highlight the additional time available for refining the work, ensuring higher quality, or addressing unforeseen issues comprehensively. This approach not only mitigates the immediate disappointment but also encourages a forward-thinking mindset among the team members.

It is essential to maintain transparency while framing the message positively. Avoid sugar-coating the truth to the point where it becomes misleading. Instead, present the facts clearly and honestly, followed by a constructive perspective. For example, if budget cuts are necessary, acknowledge the constraints but also discuss how this can lead to more efficient resource allocation or innovative problem-solving strategies. By doing so, the team can feel more motivated and less disheartened by the setback.

Active listening plays a crucial role in this process. After delivering the news, give team members the space to express their concerns and feelings. Acknowledge their emotions and validate their experiences, showing empathy and understanding. This creates a supportive environment where individuals feel heard and respected, making them more receptive to the positive framing of the message.

Another effective strategy is to involve the team in finding solutions. When people are part of the problem-solving process, they are more likely to feel a sense of ownership and responsibility, which can transform a negative situation into a collaborative effort. Encourage brainstorming sessions where everyone can contribute ideas on how to navigate the challenges. This not only fosters a sense of unity but also empowers team members to take proactive steps towards overcoming obstacles.

Timing and setting are also crucial factors. Choose a moment when the team is not under immediate stress and can give their full attention to the discussion. A calm and private setting allows for a more open and honest conversation, free from external pressures or distractions. This thoughtful approach demonstrates respect for the team and the seriousness with which the news is being treated.

Incorporating regular check-ins and updates can further reinforce the positive framing of the message. By consistently communicating progress and acknowledging small victories, a project manager can maintain morale and keep the team focused on the end goal. Celebrating milestones, no matter how minor, helps to build momentum and reinforces the idea that, despite setbacks, the project is still moving forward.

Ultimately, the key to delivering bad news effectively lies in balancing honesty with optimism. By framing the message positively, a project manager can help the team navigate through difficulties with resilience and a constructive attitude. This approach not only minimizes the immediate impact of the bad news but also fosters a culture of trust, collaboration, and continuous improvement.

Chapter 4: Delivering the News

Opening the Conversation

The air in the conference room felt heavy, thick with anticipation and the unspoken tension of impending bad news. The fluorescent lights cast a stark, almost clinical glow on the polished wooden table, around which the team members sat, their faces a mix of curiosity and concern. A project manager's role often involves navigating these murky waters, where the delivery of unfavorable updates becomes inevitable.

As the project manager, you take a deep breath, feeling the weight of the responsibility on your shoulders. The silence is palpable, each second stretching out as you prepare to break it. You know that how you open this conversation will set the tone for everything that follows. It's not just about the words you choose, but the manner in which you present them. Every gesture, every inflection in your voice, will be scrutinized and interpreted.

You begin with a nod, acknowledging the presence of each person in the room. Eye contact is crucial; it establishes a connection, a bridge of trust that you will need to cross together. Your voice, though steady, carries a softness, an empathy that you hope will cushion the blow of the news you are about to deliver.

"Thank you all for coming on such short notice," you start, your tone measured and sincere. You observe their reactions, the slight shifts in their seats, the attentive looks. It's a delicate dance, this act of communication, where every move counts. You continue, "I want to assure you that I have taken every possible measure to analyze our current situation thoroughly."

The initial statement is crucial. It must convey transparency and a sense of shared responsibility. You are not here to place blame but to navigate a challenge together. You pause, allowing the gravity of your words to sink in, giving them a moment to prepare mentally for what's to come.

"As you know, our project has faced several unexpected hurdles," you say, your eyes scanning the room, meeting theirs with unwavering honesty. "Despite our best efforts, we have encountered significant delays that will impact our delivery timeline."

The room remains silent, but you can sense the shift in energy. Some faces fall, while others remain stoic, bracing themselves for more details. You maintain your composure, understanding that this is just the beginning of a difficult conversation. The key is to stay calm, clear, and compassionate.

"Let's discuss the specifics," you continue, ensuring your voice remains even and composed. "I have detailed the issues in the report you all have in front of you. Each challenge has been documented, along with the steps we've already taken to mitigate them."

By now, you can see them flipping through the pages, their eyes scanning the text. You've provided them with the information they need, but more importantly, you've created an environment where they feel included in the process. This isn't just your burden to bear; it's a collective challenge that you will face together.

You take another breath, feeling the room's atmosphere begin to shift from one of dread to a more collaborative spirit. The conversation has been opened, the bad news delivered with care and consideration. Now, it's time to work together to find a path forward.

Being Honest and Direct

In the realm of project management, delivering bad news is an inevitable task that requires a delicate balance of honesty and directness. The ability to convey unfavorable updates effectively can significantly impact the project's trajectory and the team's morale. The essence of being honest and direct lies in the clarity and transparency with which the information is shared, ensuring that all stakeholders are fully aware of the situation without any sugar-coating or evasion.

When faced with the necessity to deliver bad news, the first step is to gather all relevant information. Understanding the full scope of the issue, its causes, and potential impacts allows the project manager to communicate more effectively. It's essential to be thorough in this preparation phase, as incomplete or inaccurate information can lead to misunderstandings and further complications.

Once equipped with the necessary details, the project manager should choose an appropriate setting for the conversation. Opting for a private and neutral environment helps to maintain confidentiality and allows for a candid dialogue. This setting also demonstrates respect for the individuals involved, acknowledging the sensitivity of the situation.

The manner in which the news is delivered is crucial. A calm and composed demeanor helps to set the tone for the discussion. It's important to be straightforward, avoiding any ambiguous language that might confuse or mislead. Using clear and concise language ensures that the message is understood without room for misinterpretation. This direct approach, while sometimes uncomfortable, is appreciated for its honesty and helps to build trust over the long term.

Acknowledging the emotional impact of the news is another critical aspect. Recognizing that the information might be disappointing or stressful for the recipients shows empathy and understanding. This acknowledgment can help to soften the blow and demonstrates that the project manager is not indifferent to the team's feelings. Providing a space for the team to express their concerns and ask questions can also be beneficial, fostering an open dialogue and allowing for a shared understanding of the situation.

Offering solutions or next steps is an integral part of delivering bad news. While the news itself might be unfavorable, presenting a clear plan of action can help to mitigate its impact. Outlining potential solutions, contingency plans, or steps to prevent future issues provides a sense of direction and can help to restore confidence. This proactive approach shows that the project manager is committed to navigating through the difficulties and is focused on finding a resolution.

Throughout the conversation, maintaining a sense of accountability is paramount. Taking responsibility for the issue, where appropriate, and being open about any mistakes or oversights, reinforces the integrity of the project manager. This honesty not only helps to build trust but also sets a precedent for the team, encouraging a culture of transparency and responsibility.

In the aftermath of delivering bad news, follow-up is essential. Checking in with the team to address any lingering concerns, provide updates on progress, and offer support helps to maintain morale and ensures that the team remains aligned with the project's objectives. This ongoing communication underscores the project manager's commitment to the team's well-being and the project's success.

In essence, being honest and direct when delivering bad news is a multifaceted approach that requires preparation, clarity, empathy, and accountability. By adhering to these principles, a project manager can navigate these challenging conversations with integrity, ultimately fostering a more resilient and cohesive team.

Managing Reactions

When tasked with delivering bad news, a project manager must be acutely aware of how their message will be received. The initial reaction from team members, stakeholders, or clients can vary widely, from shock and disappointment to anger and frustration. Understanding and managing these reactions is crucial for maintaining project cohesion and morale.

The first step is to prepare for the range of emotions that may arise. By anticipating potential reactions, a project manager can craft their message to be as empathetic and clear as possible. It's essential to recognize that each individual will process bad news differently based on their personality, role in the project, and personal stakes. Preparing responses to common questions and concerns can help in addressing the immediate emotional fallout.

During the delivery of the news, the project manager should pay close attention to non-verbal cues such as body language and facial expressions. These cues can provide valuable insight into how the news is being received, often before any verbal response is given. Maintaining eye contact, using a calm and steady tone, and showing genuine concern can help in creating a supportive atmosphere.

Active listening plays a pivotal role in managing reactions. Allowing the recipients of the news to express their feelings and thoughts without interruption can help in diffusing heightened emotions. Acknowledging their feelings with statements like "I understand this is difficult" or "I can see why you're upset" validates their emotions and shows empathy. This approach helps in building trust and can make it easier to navigate through the initial shock.

Providing a clear rationale for the bad news is also important. When people understand the reasons behind a decision or an unforeseen issue, they are more likely to accept it, even if they don't agree with it. Transparency in explaining the situation helps in reducing feelings of distrust or suspicion. It's beneficial to outline any steps that have been taken to mitigate the issue and what future actions will be implemented to prevent recurrence.

Offering support and solutions is another key aspect. People need to feel that there is a way forward, even if the current news is unfavorable. By presenting a clear plan of action or potential solutions, a project manager can help in shifting the focus from the problem to the resolution. This proactive approach can alleviate some of the immediate negative reactions and foster a sense of control over the situation.

It's also crucial to follow up after the initial conversation. Checking in with team members, stakeholders, or clients to see how they are coping with the news shows ongoing support and commitment. This follow-up can be an opportunity to address any lingering concerns and to reinforce the steps being taken to move forward.

Managing reactions effectively requires a blend of empathy, clear communication, and proactive problem-solving. By preparing for emotional responses, actively listening, providing rationale, offering support, and following up, a project manager can navigate the complexities of delivering bad news while maintaining trust and morale within the team.

Providing Solutions and Next Steps

When a project manager faces the daunting task of delivering bad news, the approach taken can significantly influence the project's trajectory. It's not just about relaying information; it's about offering a pathway forward, ensuring that stakeholders are not left in a state of despair but rather see a glimmer of hope amidst the challenges.

To begin with, after presenting the bad news, it is crucial to immediately pivot towards potential solutions. This shift in focus helps to mitigate the initial shock and provides a sense of direction. A project manager must come prepared with a well-thought-out plan that addresses the core issues at hand. This plan should include a detailed analysis of the problem, potential solutions, and the rationale behind each option. The more comprehensive and transparent the plan, the more likely it is to gain stakeholder buy-in.

In this phase, collaboration becomes a key element. Engaging the team and stakeholders in brainstorming sessions can unearth innovative solutions that might not have been considered otherwise. By fostering an environment where everyone feels their input is valued, a project manager can build a collective sense of ownership over the resolution process. This collaborative approach not only enhances the quality of the solutions but also strengthens team cohesion.

Once potential solutions are identified, it's essential to outline the next steps clearly. This involves creating a detailed action plan with specific, measurable, achievable, relevant, and time-bound (SMART) goals. Each task should be assigned to a responsible party, with deadlines that are realistic yet ambitious enough to maintain momentum. Clear communication of these steps ensures that all stakeholders are aligned and understand their roles in the recovery process.

Transparency remains paramount throughout this stage. Regular updates on progress, challenges, and any adjustments to the plan are necessary to maintain trust and keep everyone informed. A project manager should establish a consistent communication schedule, leveraging various tools and platforms to ensure that information is disseminated effectively. This could include status meetings, progress reports, and dashboards that provide real-time updates.

Another critical aspect is managing expectations. It's important to be honest about what can realistically be achieved and the potential risks involved. Overpromising and underdelivering can further erode trust and morale. By setting realistic expectations and delivering on them, a project manager can rebuild confidence and demonstrate reliability.

Moreover, contingency planning should not be overlooked. Preparing for potential setbacks by having a plan B (and even a plan C) can help navigate unforeseen challenges without derailing the entire project. This proactive approach shows foresight and preparedness, which can reassure stakeholders that the project is in capable hands.

Empathy and support also play a significant role in this phase. Acknowledging the emotional impact of the bad news and offering support can help alleviate some of the stress and anxiety that stakeholders may feel. This human element is often overlooked but can be incredibly powerful in maintaining morale and fostering a positive working environment.

Ultimately, the goal is to transform a negative situation into an opportunity for growth and improvement. By providing viable solutions and a clear roadmap for moving forward, a project manager can turn bad news into a catalyst for positive change, demonstrating resilience and leadership in the face of adversity.

Chapter 5: Handling Different Stakeholders

Communicating with Team Members

Navigating the delicate task of delivering bad news to team members requires a blend of empathy, clarity, and strategic communication skills. As a project manager, understanding the nuances of your team's dynamics and individual personalities is crucial in ensuring that the news is received in a constructive manner. The primary goal is to maintain morale and productivity while fostering a culture of transparency and trust.

When preparing to deliver unfortunate news, timing is a pivotal factor. Choosing the right moment can significantly influence how the information is perceived and processed. For instance, delivering bad news at the end of the workday allows team members to digest the information without the immediate pressure of ongoing tasks. However, this approach might also lead to anxiety and unrest outside of work hours. Conversely, addressing the issue early in the day can provide time for discussion and resolution but might impact productivity. Striking a balance based on the specific context and the severity of the news is essential.

The setting in which the news is delivered also plays a significant role. Opting for a private, quiet space ensures that the conversation remains confidential and respectful. This environment allows team members to express their concerns and emotions freely, without the fear of judgment from their peers. It is important to approach the situation with a calm demeanor, demonstrating that you are in control and prepared to support your team through the difficult period.

Crafting the message with care is equally important. Start by acknowledging the efforts and contributions of the team, which helps to soften the blow and shows appreciation for their hard work. Use clear and straightforward language to convey the bad news, avoiding jargon or technical terms that might confuse or alienate team members. Be honest about the situation, providing as much context as possible without overwhelming them with unnecessary details. Transparency fosters trust, even in challenging times.

Empathy is a key component in these conversations. Recognize and validate the emotions of your team members, whether it's disappointment, frustration, or concern. Allow them the space to express their feelings and ask questions. Active listening is crucial; it demonstrates that you value their input and are committed to addressing their concerns. Offer reassurance by outlining the steps you plan to take to mitigate the impact of the bad news and involve the team in problem-solving where appropriate. This collaborative approach can help to rebuild confidence and a sense of control.

Follow-up is another critical aspect of delivering bad news. After the initial conversation, provide regular updates on any developments and remain available for further discussions. This ongoing communication helps to reinforce your commitment to transparency and support. Additionally, recognize the efforts of team members who demonstrate resilience and adaptability in the face of adversity. Positive reinforcement can significantly boost morale and encourage a proactive attitude.

In situations where the news might have a broader impact, consider preparing additional resources such as counseling services or professional development opportunities. These can provide valuable support to team members, helping them to navigate the emotional and professional challenges that arise from the situation.

Effectively communicating bad news to team members is a delicate balancing act that requires sensitivity, clarity, and a strategic approach. By prioritizing empathy, transparency, and ongoing support, a project manager can help to maintain trust and morale, even in the most challenging circumstances.

Addressing Upper Management

Navigating the delicate task of delivering bad news to upper management demands a blend of tact, clarity, and empathy. The stakes are high, as the repercussions of the news can impact strategic decisions, company morale, and even the organization's bottom line. Therefore, the project manager must approach this task with a well-thought-out strategy.

Upper management often has a limited amount of time and a vast array of responsibilities, so the delivery of bad news must be concise and to the point. Begin by clearly stating the issue at hand. Avoid sugar-coating or downplaying the severity of the problem, as this can lead to misunderstandings and a lack of trust. Use precise language and provide specific examples to illustrate the issue. This not only helps in painting a clear picture but also demonstrates that the project manager has a firm grasp of the situation.

It is crucial to anticipate the questions and concerns that upper management might have. Prepare detailed answers and have supporting data readily available. This preparation shows a proactive approach and reassures upper management that the project manager is in control, even in challenging circumstances. Moreover, it is beneficial to present a well-structured plan to address the problem. Outline the steps that have been taken so far, what will be done moving forward, and how these actions will mitigate the issue. This demonstrates a commitment to resolving the problem and instills confidence in the project manager's capability.

Empathy plays a vital role in these interactions. Acknowledge the potential impact of the bad news on the company's objectives and express an understanding of the concerns upper management may have. This fosters a sense of partnership and shared responsibility. It is also important to listen actively to their feedback and suggestions, showing that their input is valued and considered in the problem-solving process.

While it is essential to be honest about the severity of the situation, it is equally important to highlight any positive aspects or opportunities that may arise from addressing the issue. This could include lessons learned, potential improvements in processes, or any early signs of recovery. Balancing the bad news with constructive elements can help maintain a forward-looking perspective and motivate the team to overcome the challenge.

Non-verbal communication also plays a significant role in these interactions. Maintain eye contact, use a calm and steady tone of voice, and exhibit open body language. These cues convey confidence and sincerity, helping to build trust and rapport with upper management. Additionally, choosing the right setting for delivering the news is crucial. A private, quiet environment free from distractions allows for a focused and respectful conversation.

The timing of the communication is another critical factor. Deliver the news as soon as it is feasible, allowing upper management ample time to react and make informed decisions. Delaying the communication can exacerbate the problem and erode trust. However, ensure that the information is accurate and that all necessary details have been gathered before initiating the conversation.

In these challenging moments, the project manager's ability to convey bad news effectively can significantly influence the outcome. By being direct, prepared, empathetic, and maintaining open lines of communication, the project manager can navigate this difficult task with professionalism and integrity, ultimately fostering a culture of transparency and trust within the organization.

Informing Clients and Customers

Delivering bad news to clients and customers is a delicate task that requires a blend of empathy, clarity, and professionalism. The approach must be meticulously planned to maintain trust and keep the relationship intact. The first step is to ensure a thorough understanding of the situation. A project manager must gather all relevant information, including the cause of the issue, its impact, and potential solutions. This preparation provides a solid foundation for the conversation, enabling the manager to address concerns confidently and accurately.

Timing is critical. Bad news should be communicated as soon as it is confirmed, but not before all facts are verified. Delaying the delivery can exacerbate the situation and erode trust. Clients and customers appreciate honesty and transparency. It is essential to choose an appropriate setting for the conversation, one that ensures privacy and allows for an uninterrupted discussion. Face-to-face meetings are preferable, as they allow for a more personal connection and enable the project manager to gauge reactions and respond accordingly. If an in-person meeting is not possible, video calls are the next best option.

The manner in which the news is delivered is just as important as the content of the message. A calm and composed demeanor helps to reassure clients and customers, even when the news is unfavorable. Start with a brief overview of the project's progress to provide context, then clearly and concisely explain the issue. Avoid technical jargon that might confuse or alienate the audience. Instead, use straightforward language that conveys the gravity of the situation without causing unnecessary alarm.

Empathy plays a crucial role in these conversations. Acknowledge the impact of the bad news on the client or customer and express genuine regret. Phrases like "I understand this is disappointing" or "I apologize for the inconvenience this has caused" can help to humanize the situation and demonstrate that their concerns are taken seriously. It is important to listen actively to their responses and questions, showing that their perspective is valued.

Offering solutions or alternatives is a key component of delivering bad news. Presenting a well-thought-out plan to address the issue can help to mitigate the negative impact and demonstrate a commitment to finding a resolution. Be prepared to discuss the steps that will be taken to prevent similar issues in the future. This proactive approach not only addresses the immediate problem but also reassures clients and customers that measures are in place to safeguard against future occurrences.

Follow-up is essential. After the initial conversation, send a summary of the discussion and the agreed-upon action plan. This reinforces the message and provides a reference point for both parties. Regular updates on the progress of the resolution process help to maintain transparency and keep clients and customers informed. This ongoing communication is vital in rebuilding trust and demonstrating accountability.

In essence, the process of informing clients and customers about bad news involves a careful balance of honesty, empathy, and proactive problem-solving. By approaching the situation with a well-prepared plan, clear communication, and a focus on solutions, a project manager can navigate the challenging task of delivering unfavorable news while preserving the integrity of the professional relationship.

Dealing with External Partners

Managing relationships with external partners is a delicate aspect of project management, particularly when it comes to delivering unfavorable news. The dynamics of these relationships can be complex, as they often involve multiple stakeholders, contractual obligations, and varying expectations. Navigating this landscape requires a blend of tact, transparency, and strategic communication.

The first step in addressing external partners is to understand their perspective. External partners typically have their own set of goals, constraints, and pressures. Recognizing these factors can help in framing the message in a way that acknowledges their situation. It's important to conduct a thorough analysis of the potential impact of the bad news on their operations and to anticipate their concerns and questions.

Preparation is crucial. Before initiating the conversation, gather all relevant information and evidence that supports the bad news. This could include data, reports, timelines, and any other documentation that provides a clear picture of the situation. Having this information at hand demonstrates thoroughness and helps in building credibility.

Choosing the right medium for communication is another critical decision. While emails and written reports might suffice for minor issues, significant setbacks or delays are best communicated through direct conversations, whether in-person or via video conferencing. This approach allows for immediate feedback, clarifications, and a more personal touch, which can be vital in maintaining trust and goodwill.

When delivering the news, clarity and honesty are paramount. It is essential to articulate the problem succinctly, avoiding jargon or technical language that might obscure the message. Explain what has happened, why it has happened, and what the implications are. Being straightforward about the situation helps in managing expectations and reduces the likelihood of misunderstandings.

Empathy plays a significant role in these interactions. Acknowledge the inconvenience or challenges the bad news may cause for the external partner. Expressing genuine regret and understanding can go a long way in softening the blow. Phrases like "I understand this is not the news you were hoping for" or "We recognize the impact this may have on your timeline" can help in conveying empathy.

It is equally important to present a plan of action alongside the bad news. Outline the steps being taken to address the issue, mitigate the impact, and prevent similar occurrences in the future. Providing a clear path forward demonstrates proactive problem-solving and reassures the external partner that the situation is being managed diligently.

Encouraging a two-way dialogue is beneficial. Invite the external partner to share their thoughts, concerns, and suggestions. This collaborative approach can lead to more effective solutions and fosters a sense of partnership rather than a transactional relationship. It also provides an opportunity to address any immediate questions or misconceptions.

Follow-up is a crucial component of the process. After the initial conversation, ensure that there are regular updates on the progress being made to resolve the issue. Consistent communication helps in maintaining transparency and reinforces the commitment to finding a resolution.

In dealing with external partners, the goal is to maintain a balance between honesty and sensitivity. Delivering bad news is never easy, but with careful preparation, empathetic communication, and a focus on solutions, it is possible to manage these situations effectively and maintain positive working relationships.

Chapter 6: Maintaining Morale and Motivation

Recognizing Team Emotions

Understanding the emotional landscape of your team is crucial when delivering bad news. As a project manager, you must be able to sense the subtle shifts in mood and energy that can occur when a project hits a snag or when expectations are not met. The ability to recognize and address these emotional cues can make a significant difference in how the news is received and how the team moves forward.

One of the first signs of emotional change in a team is often non-verbal. Body language can speak volumes before a single word is spoken. Slumped shoulders, lack of eye contact, and sighs of frustration are all indicators that your team might be bracing for disappointment. Paying close attention to these signals allows you to gauge the emotional temperature of the room. It's essential to create an environment where team members feel safe expressing their emotions, whether through a furrowed brow or a hesitant question.

Active listening is another critical tool in recognizing team emotions. When team members voice their concerns, frustrations, or fears, it's important to listen without interruption. This not only validates their feelings but also provides you with valuable insights into the emotional undercurrents affecting the team. Reflecting back what you've heard by summarizing their points shows empathy and understanding, which can help in alleviating some of the emotional burden they might be carrying.

The tone of voice is another significant indicator of emotional states. A normally enthusiastic team member who suddenly speaks in a monotone or a quiet voice may be signaling distress or disappointment. Conversely, raised voices or heated tones can indicate anger or frustration. Recognizing these changes in vocal patterns can help you identify who might need more support or a private conversation to air their feelings.

Another aspect to consider is the overall morale and energy level of the team. A once vibrant and collaborative group that now seems disengaged or disinterested likely indicates a collective emotional downturn. This could be due to a variety of factors, including stress, burnout, or a sense of impending failure. Keeping a pulse on the team's general mood can help you intervene before negative emotions spiral out of control.

Regular check-ins and one-on-one meetings can provide deeper insights into individual emotional states. These settings allow for more candid conversations where team members might feel more comfortable sharing their true feelings. Asking open-ended questions like, "How are you feeling about the project's progress?" or "Is there anything that's been particularly challenging for you lately?" can elicit more than just surface-level responses.

It's also important to be aware of your own emotions and how they might impact the team. As a leader, your emotional state can influence the entire group. If you're visibly stressed or anxious, your team is likely to pick up on that and mirror those emotions. Striving for emotional intelligence and self-awareness can help you manage your own reactions and set a more positive tone for the team.

Creating a culture of transparency and open communication can also make it easier to recognize and address emotions. When team members feel that they can speak openly without fear of retribution, they are more likely to share their true feelings. This openness can lead to a more supportive and cohesive team environment, even when faced with challenging news.

Recognizing and understanding team emotions is not just about identifying negative feelings but also about celebrating positive ones. Acknowledging small victories and expressing gratitude can boost morale and create a more resilient team. Balancing the emotional scales in this way can make the task of delivering bad news a little less daunting.

By honing your ability to recognize and address the emotional states of your team, you can navigate the complexities of delivering bad news with greater empathy and effectiveness. This skill not only helps in managing the immediate impact of the news but also in fostering a stronger, more emotionally intelligent team in the long run.

Encouraging Open Dialogue

A project manager's role entails not only overseeing tasks and ensuring deadlines are met but also communicating effectively, including when the news isn't favorable. The ability to encourage open dialogue can make a significant difference in how bad news is received and managed. Cultivating an environment where team members feel comfortable expressing concerns, asking questions, and providing feedback can transform potentially negative situations into opportunities for growth and improvement.

An open dialogue begins with establishing a foundation of trust. The project manager must be approachable and consistently demonstrate integrity and transparency. When team members see that their leader is honest and upfront, they are more likely to reciprocate that behavior. This mutual trust is crucial when delivering bad news, as it reassures the team that even unfavorable updates are shared with their best interests in mind.

Creating a safe space for communication is also essential. Team members need to feel that their opinions are valued and that they won't face repercussions for speaking up. This can be fostered by actively listening to their concerns, acknowledging their input, and ensuring that their voices are heard. Regular check-ins and open forums can provide structured opportunities for team members to share their thoughts and feelings without fear of judgment.

The language and tone used by the project manager play a pivotal role in encouraging open dialogue. It's important to communicate with empathy and understanding, recognizing the impact that bad news can have on the team. Using inclusive language and avoiding blame can help create a more supportive atmosphere. Phrases like "We are facing a challenge" or "We need to find a solution together" can foster a sense of unity and collective responsibility.

Non-verbal communication is equally important. Maintaining eye contact, nodding in agreement, and displaying open body language can signal to team members that their input is valued.

These subtle cues can help build rapport and make team members feel more at ease when discussing difficult topics.

Encouraging open dialogue also involves being receptive to feedback. A project manager needs to be willing to listen to criticism and consider alternative viewpoints. This openness can lead to more effective problem-solving and demonstrate to the team that their perspectives are respected. By showing that feedback is taken seriously and acted upon, a project manager can build a culture of continuous improvement.

It's also beneficial to establish clear communication channels. Whether through regular team meetings, one-on-one sessions, or digital platforms, having defined avenues for discussion can ensure that important information is shared promptly and effectively. These channels should be accessible and user-friendly, allowing team members to communicate comfortably and efficiently.

Recognizing and addressing emotions is another key aspect. Bad news can evoke a range of emotional responses, and it's important for the project manager to acknowledge these feelings. Offering support and understanding can help mitigate the negative impact and foster a more resilient team. Providing resources, such as counseling services or stress management workshops, can further support team members during challenging times.

By fostering an environment of open dialogue, a project manager can turn the delivery of bad news into a collaborative effort. This approach not only helps in managing the immediate situation but also strengthens the team's cohesion and resilience in the long run. Through trust, empathy, and effective communication, a project manager can navigate the complexities of delivering bad news while maintaining a positive and productive team dynamic.

Fostering a Supportive Environment

Creating an atmosphere of trust and mutual respect is essential for a project manager tasked with delivering bad news. The environment in which such news is shared can significantly influence how the information is received and processed by the team. Establishing this supportive environment starts long before any difficult conversations take place.

A project manager can lay the groundwork by promoting open communication within the team. This involves encouraging team members to share their thoughts, concerns, and feedback without fear of retribution. Regular check-ins, both formal and informal, help to build this culture of openness. During these interactions, active listening is key. A project manager should not only hear but also understand the viewpoints and emotions of their team members, validating their feelings and showing empathy.

Transparency is another cornerstone of a supportive environment. Keeping the team informed about project developments, both good and bad, fosters a sense of inclusiveness and trust. When team members feel that they are kept in the loop, they are more likely to respond constructively to negative news. Moreover, being transparent about potential risks and challenges from the outset prepares the team for possible setbacks, making the eventual delivery of bad news less shocking.

Building personal connections with team members also contributes to a supportive atmosphere. Taking the time to know each individual, their strengths, weaknesses, and personal circumstances, allows a project manager to tailor their approach when delivering bad news. This personalized attention demonstrates that the project manager values them not just as employees, but as individuals, further strengthening the bond of trust.

The physical setting in which bad news is delivered can also impact the reception. Choosing a private, comfortable space where team members can express their reactions freely is crucial. This consideration shows respect for their feelings and provides a safe space for open dialogue. Ensuring that such conversations are free from interruptions reinforces the seriousness and respect with which the project manager treats the situation.

Timing plays a significant role as well. Delivering bad news at an appropriate time, when team members are more likely to be receptive and less distracted by other pressures, can make a substantial difference. Avoiding end-of-day or pre-weekend meetings helps prevent prolonged anxiety and allows for a more immediate resolution-focused discussion.

Empathy is a powerful tool in these situations. A project manager should acknowledge the emotional impact of the news and provide support. This could include offering solutions, discussing next steps, or simply allowing time for the team to process the information. Demonstrating understanding and compassion helps to mitigate the negative impact and fosters a sense of solidarity.

Encouraging a culture of resilience and problem-solving is also beneficial. When team members are accustomed to facing challenges together and finding solutions, they are better equipped to handle bad news. This proactive approach turns potentially demoralizing situations into opportunities for growth and improvement.

By fostering a supportive environment, a project manager not only eases the process of delivering bad news but also strengthens the team's overall cohesion and resilience. This environment of trust, transparency, and empathy ensures that even in the face of setbacks, the team remains motivated and united, ready to tackle the challenges ahead.

Celebrating Small Wins

Amid the myriad challenges and complexities that a project manager faces, there lies an often-overlooked yet profoundly impactful strategy: the celebration of small wins. Acknowledging these minor victories can serve as a powerful antidote to the inevitable moments when bad news must be delivered. These celebrations not only boost team morale but also create a culture of positivity and resilience, essential for navigating the turbulent waters of project management.

Imagine a scenario where a project is running behind schedule, and the team is feeling the weight of impending deadlines. The atmosphere is tense, and the looming necessity to convey disappointing news to stakeholders adds to the pressure. In such a context, recognizing and celebrating small achievements can act as a beacon of hope. It's about taking a moment to appreciate the incremental progress made, despite the larger obstacles. This could be as simple as acknowledging a team member who stayed late to troubleshoot an issue or celebrating the completion of a critical but minor milestone.

These small celebrations do not require grand gestures. They can be as modest as a shout-out in a team meeting, a thank-you email, or a quick coffee break together. The essence lies in the recognition and validation of effort and progress. This practice fosters a sense of accomplishment and encourages a growth mindset, where the focus is on continuous improvement rather than solely on the end goal. It shifts the narrative from one of impending doom to one of ongoing achievement.

Moreover, celebrating small wins can have a ripple effect on team dynamics. It cultivates an environment where team members feel valued and motivated. This positive reinforcement can enhance collaboration and drive, making it easier to tackle the larger challenges that lie ahead. When individuals know that their efforts, no matter how small, are noticed and appreciated, they are more likely to maintain high levels of engagement and productivity.

For the project manager, this approach also serves as a strategic tool for communicating bad news. When a team is accustomed to regular recognition of their hard work, they are more resilient and better prepared to handle setbacks. The project manager can frame the bad news within the context of the progress that has been made, emphasizing the team's strengths and the victories they have achieved along the way. This balanced perspective can mitigate the negative impact of the bad news and maintain the team's morale and focus.

Additionally, celebrating small wins helps build trust and transparency within the team. It demonstrates that the project manager is attentive to the team's efforts and is committed to their well-being. This trust is crucial when delivering bad news, as it ensures that the team remains cohesive and supportive, rather than becoming disheartened or divided.

In the broader scope of project management, the practice of celebrating small wins can also enhance stakeholder relationships. Regular updates that highlight these minor victories can keep stakeholders engaged and informed, providing a more nuanced understanding of the project's progress. This transparency can ease the process of delivering bad news, as stakeholders are more likely to appreciate the context and the continuous efforts being made.

Thus, the celebration of small wins is not merely a morale-boosting tactic but a strategic approach that can significantly influence the overall success of a project. It creates a resilient and motivated team, fosters a positive and transparent culture, and provides a balanced framework for communicating both good and bad news. In the intricate dance of project management, these small celebrations can make a world of difference, transforming challenges into opportunities for growth and learning.

Chapter 7: Learning from the Experience

Conducting Post-Mortem Analysis

In the aftermath of any project, especially those that have not met expectations, a post-mortem analysis becomes an essential tool for growth and learning. This reflective process delves into the intricacies of what transpired, aiming to uncover the root causes of failures and to identify areas for improvement. The role of the project manager in this scenario is pivotal, as they must navigate the delicate balance of delivering candid feedback while fostering a constructive atmosphere.

The first step in conducting a post-mortem analysis involves gathering all relevant data and documentation from the project. This encompasses timelines, budgets, communication logs, and any other pertinent records that can shed light on the project's progression. By meticulously reviewing these documents, the project manager can piece together a comprehensive timeline of events, pinpointing where deviations from the plan occurred.

Engaging the project team in open and honest discussions is crucial. These debriefing sessions should be conducted in a non-judgmental environment, where team members feel safe to express their thoughts and perspectives. Encouraging transparency and fostering an atmosphere of trust are key to obtaining genuine insights. It is important for the project manager to actively listen, acknowledging both the successes and the shortcomings experienced by the team.

Identifying the specific factors that contributed to the project's outcome is a nuanced task. This involves distinguishing between internal and external influences, as well as recognizing both controllable and uncontrollable elements. Internal factors may include team dynamics, resource allocation, and decision-making processes, while external factors could encompass market conditions, stakeholder expectations, or unforeseen events. By categorizing these influences, the project manager can better understand the interplay of various elements that impacted the project.

Analysing the data and feedback collected, the project manager should look for patterns and recurring themes. These patterns often reveal underlying issues that may have been overlooked during the project's execution. For instance, repeated communication breakdowns might indicate a need for improved channels or protocols. Similarly, recurring delays could suggest flaws in the planning or estimation phases. By identifying these patterns, the project manager can pinpoint systemic issues that require attention.

Developing actionable recommendations is the next critical step. These recommendations should be specific, measurable, and achievable, providing a clear roadmap for future projects. It is essential to focus on solutions that can be realistically implemented, taking into account the available resources and constraints. The project manager should prioritize these recommendations based on their potential impact and feasibility, ensuring that the most critical areas are addressed first.

Communicating the findings and recommendations to stakeholders is a delicate task. The project manager must present the information in a balanced manner, highlighting both the lessons learned and the steps being taken to prevent similar issues in the future. This communication should be transparent and constructive, aiming to build confidence and trust among stakeholders. It is important to frame the discussion in a way that emphasizes continuous improvement and the commitment to learning from past experiences.

Documenting the entire post-mortem process is essential for future reference. This documentation serves as a valuable resource for the organization, providing insights and guidance for future projects. By maintaining a repository of post-mortem reports, the organization can track progress over time and continuously refine its project management practices.

Conducting a thorough post-mortem analysis not only helps in understanding the factors that led to a project's outcome but also fosters a culture of continuous improvement. Through careful examination and open dialogue, project managers can turn setbacks into valuable learning opportunities, ultimately enhancing their ability to deliver successful projects in the future.

Identifying Areas for Improvement

Understanding the delicate nuances of delivering bad news is a crucial skill for any project manager. Before addressing the delivery itself, it's essential to pinpoint the areas where improvement is needed. This phase involves a keen sense of observation, an analytic mindset, and the ability to gather and interpret data accurately.

To start, a project manager must immerse themselves in the project's details. This means delving into the current state of the project, assessing timelines, budgets, and resource allocations. By scrutinizing these elements, one can identify discrepancies between the planned objectives and the actual progress. This step is not just about spotting what went wrong, but understanding the root causes behind these deviations.

Engaging with the team is another critical aspect. Regular check-ins and open lines of communication allow a project manager to gauge the team's morale and performance. These interactions can reveal underlying issues such as workload imbalances, skill mismatches, or interpersonal conflicts. Listening to team members' concerns and suggestions provides invaluable insights that might not be evident through data alone.

In addition to internal factors, external influences must also be considered. Market trends, stakeholder expectations, and regulatory changes can all impact a project's trajectory. Keeping a finger on the pulse of these external elements helps in understanding how they may have contributed to the current situation. This broader perspective ensures that no stone is left unturned in the quest for improvement.

Analyzing past projects can also shed light on recurring patterns or pitfalls. By reviewing previous outcomes, a project manager can identify common themes that may be affecting current performance. This historical analysis serves as a learning tool, helping to avoid repeating the same mistakes and to build on past successes.

Feedback from stakeholders is another vital component. Their perspectives can highlight areas that might not be immediately apparent to the project team. Stakeholders often have a different vantage point, focusing on the project's impact and alignment with broader organizational goals. Their input can help in identifying strategic misalignments or overlooked opportunities.

Once the areas for improvement have been identified, the next step is to prioritize them. Not all issues will have the same level of impact on the project. Determining which problems are most critical and addressing them first ensures that resources are allocated efficiently and effectively. This prioritization process involves weighing the potential benefits of resolving each issue against the effort and resources required.

Documenting these findings is crucial. A clear, concise report that outlines the identified areas for improvement, along with supporting data and analysis, provides a solid foundation for the next steps. This documentation serves as a reference point for discussions with stakeholders and as a guide for the team's corrective actions.

In this meticulous process of identifying areas for improvement, a project manager must balance objectivity with empathy. Recognizing the human element behind the data is essential. It's not just about numbers and charts, but also about understanding the challenges faced by the team and the stakeholders. This holistic approach ensures that the path to improvement is not only effective but also considerate of the people involved.

By thoroughly identifying areas for improvement, a project manager sets the stage for delivering bad news in a constructive manner. This groundwork ensures that the subsequent communication is grounded in a deep understanding of the project's current state and the steps needed to move forward.

Implementing Lessons Learned

The process of delivering bad news as a project manager is a multifaceted challenge that requires not just communication skills but also the wisdom to learn from past experiences. The essence of effectively handling such situations lies in the ability to reflect on previous encounters and extracting valuable insights that can be applied to future scenarios. This approach ensures that each difficult conversation becomes a stepping stone toward better management and communication practices.

Imagine a scenario where a project manager has just navigated through a particularly tough project phase, marred by delays and unforeseen complications. The team is disheartened, stakeholders are frustrated, and the manager has had to deliver disappointing updates more frequently than anyone would like. This is the crucible where lessons are forged. The manager must take a step back and methodically analyze what transpired. What were the root causes of the delays? Were there warning signs that were missed? How did the communication strategies employed either alleviate or exacerbate the situation?

Once these questions are answered, the next step is to document these lessons meticulously. A well-organized repository of lessons learned serves as a valuable reference. This documentation should be detailed, highlighting not only the mistakes but also the successful tactics that mitigated the impact of bad news. It should be a living document, regularly updated and easily accessible to the entire team.

The true test of learning, however, lies in implementation. The project manager must integrate these lessons into the planning and execution phases of subsequent projects. This might involve revising risk management strategies, enhancing communication plans, or even rethinking team dynamics and roles. For instance, if a previous project suffered due to poor risk assessment, the manager might introduce more rigorous risk identification and mitigation processes. This proactive approach can prevent similar issues from arising and prepare the team to handle them more effectively if they do.

Moreover, it is crucial to foster a culture of continuous improvement within the team. Encouraging open dialogue and feedback can help identify potential pitfalls early and create a sense of shared responsibility. Team members should feel empowered to voice concerns and suggest improvements without fear of retribution. This collective wisdom can be invaluable in refining processes and ensuring that the burden of delivering bad news does not fall solely on the manager's shoulders.

Training and development also play a significant role. Regular workshops and training sessions on communication skills, emotional intelligence, and conflict resolution can equip team members with the tools they need to handle difficult situations more gracefully. A well-prepared team can collectively manage the pressure of bad news, making the overall impact less severe.

In the end, the goal is to transform every setback into a learning opportunity. By systematically analyzing past experiences, documenting insights, and implementing changes, a project manager can build a resilient framework for future projects. This not only improves the chances of project success but also enhances the ability to deliver bad news in a way that is constructive and less damaging to team morale and stakeholder relationships. The journey of a project manager is one of perpetual learning and adaptation, where each challenge encountered is a lesson in disguise, waiting to be unraveled and utilized for future triumphs.

Documenting the Process

The role of a project manager often involves navigating through a labyrinth of complex tasks and unforeseen challenges. Among these, the delicate art of delivering bad news stands out as one of the most daunting. To effectively manage this task, it becomes imperative to document the entire process meticulously. This ensures transparency, fosters trust, and provides a clear record that can be referred back to as needed.

The foundation of effective documentation lies in understanding the significance of each phase of the project. From the initial planning stages to the final execution, every step should be recorded with precision. This involves not only noting down the successes but also the setbacks and the reasons behind them. When bad news needs to be delivered, having a comprehensive record can help in presenting the information in a clear and factual manner, devoid of ambiguities.

Maintaining a detailed log of all communications is a key aspect. Every meeting, email exchange, and phone conversation should be documented. This helps in creating a timeline of events that led to the current situation. For instance, if a delay is inevitable due to a supplier's failure to deliver materials on time, having documented evidence of all interactions with the supplier can substantiate the reasons behind the delay. This level of detail not only provides clarity but also helps in defending decisions made during the project.

Another critical element is the inclusion of risk assessments and mitigation plans. Documenting potential risks at the outset and updating these assessments as the project progresses can provide a clear picture of what was anticipated and what was unforeseen. When bad news has to be conveyed, referring to these documents can help in explaining why certain risks materialized despite the best efforts to mitigate them. This proactive approach can help in demonstrating due diligence and thorough planning.

Financial records also play a crucial role in the documentation process. Keeping track of the budget, expenditures, and any financial discrepancies can provide a transparent view of the project's financial health. If budget overruns occur, having a detailed financial record can help in pinpointing where and why the overspend happened. This transparency can be crucial when explaining financial setbacks to stakeholders.

Visual aids such as charts, graphs, and timelines can significantly enhance the documentation. These tools can help in presenting complex information in a more digestible format. For instance, a Gantt chart can visually represent the project timeline, highlighting the phases that are on track and those that are delayed. When delivering bad news, these visual aids can help in making the information more accessible and understandable.

Incorporating feedback loops into the documentation process is also essential. Regularly seeking and recording feedback from team members and stakeholders can provide valuable insights. This not only helps in identifying potential issues early but also demonstrates a commitment to continuous improvement. When issues arise, referring to documented feedback can help in showing that concerns were acknowledged and addressed to the best extent possible.

Finally, it is important to ensure that all documentation is stored in an organized and accessible manner. Using digital tools and project management software can streamline this process, making it easier to update and retrieve documents as needed. This organized approach ensures that when bad news needs to be delivered, all necessary information is readily available, providing a solid foundation for the discussion.

In essence, thorough documentation is not just about keeping records; it is about creating a comprehensive narrative of the project's journey. This narrative can be invaluable when navigating the challenging task of delivering bad news, providing clarity, transparency, and a factual basis for the conversation.

Chapter 8: Building Resilience

Developing Coping Strategies

The role of a project manager often involves navigating the tumultuous waters of unforeseen challenges and setbacks. Among the myriad duties, delivering bad news stands out as one of the most daunting tasks. It requires not only a strategic approach but also emotional resilience and tact. The ability to develop effective coping strategies becomes essential in these moments, allowing the project manager to maintain professionalism and composure.

When faced with the necessity of delivering unfavorable updates, the initial emotional response can be overwhelming. Anxiety, fear, and apprehension are common reactions that can cloud judgment and hinder effective communication. To mitigate these feelings, project managers must first acknowledge their emotions and understand that these are natural responses to difficult situations. Awareness of one's emotional state is the foundation upon which coping strategies are built.

One effective method to manage these emotions is through mindfulness practices. Techniques such as deep breathing, meditation, or even a brief moment of silence can help in centering oneself. By taking a step back and calming the mind, the project manager can approach the situation with a clearer, more focused mindset. This mental clarity is crucial for articulating the message in a manner that is both compassionate and direct.

Preparation is another key element in developing coping strategies. Thoroughly understanding the context and implications of the bad news allows the project manager to anticipate potential questions and concerns. This involves gathering all relevant information, analyzing the impact, and considering various perspectives. Armed with comprehensive knowledge, the project manager can present the news with confidence and provide well-informed answers, which helps in alleviating some of the immediate stress associated with the task

Communicating bad news is not solely about the content but also about the delivery. The tone, body language, and choice of words play significant roles in how the message is received. Practicing the delivery, perhaps in front of a mirror or with a trusted colleague, can be immensely beneficial. This rehearsal helps in refining the approach, ensuring that the message is conveyed with the appropriate level of empathy and professionalism.

Another important aspect of coping is seeking support. Project managers do not have to bear the burden alone. Engaging with mentors, peers, or even professional counselors can provide much-needed emotional support and practical advice. Sharing experiences and discussing strategies with others who have faced similar situations can offer new perspectives and coping mechanisms. This network of support can be a valuable resource in maintaining emotional well-being.

Maintaining a positive outlook, even in the face of adversity, is a powerful coping strategy. It involves recognizing that setbacks are an inevitable part of any project and viewing them as opportunities for growth and learning. By focusing on potential solutions and the steps that can be taken to mitigate the impact, the project manager can shift the narrative from one of despair to one of proactive problem-solving.

Incorporating these coping strategies into daily practice can significantly enhance a project manager's ability to handle difficult conversations. It requires a combination of emotional intelligence, preparation, and support systems. By developing these skills, project managers can navigate the challenges of delivering bad news with greater confidence and resilience, ultimately fostering a more constructive and empathetic project environment.

Promoting Mental Health and Wellbeing

In the intricate realm of project management, where deadlines loom large and expectations run high, the mental health and wellbeing of both the project manager and their team can often be overlooked. The role of a project manager is fraught with pressures that can take a toll on mental health. Acknowledging this reality is the first step toward fostering an environment where wellbeing is prioritized.

Creating a supportive atmosphere begins with open communication. Encouraging team members to express their concerns and anxieties without fear of judgment can significantly alleviate stress. Regular check-ins, whether through one-on-one meetings or team discussions, allow for the identification of potential issues before they escalate. These interactions should be approached with empathy, recognizing that everyone experiences stress differently and may have unique coping mechanisms.

Moreover, establishing clear boundaries between work and personal life is crucial. In the age of constant connectivity, it is easy for work to seep into personal time, leading to burnout. Project managers should lead by example, respecting their own time off and encouraging their team to do the same. This can be achieved by setting specific work hours, minimizing after-hours communication, and promoting the use of vacation time.

The physical workspace also plays a vital role in mental wellbeing. A cluttered, chaotic environment can contribute to feelings of overwhelm. Ensuring that the workspace is organized, with designated areas for collaboration and quiet work, can help create a sense of order and calm. Additionally, incorporating elements such as natural light, plants, and comfortable seating can enhance the overall atmosphere, making it more conducive to productivity and mental clarity.

Another important aspect is fostering a culture of recognition and appreciation. Acknowledging the hard work and achievements of team members can boost morale and motivation. This can be done through formal recognition programs or simple gestures like expressing gratitude in team meetings. Feeling valued and appreciated can significantly impact an individual's mental health, reducing feelings of stress and increasing job satisfaction.

Training and resources on stress management and mental health should also be made readily available. Workshops, seminars, or even online courses can equip team members with the tools they need to manage stress effectively. Providing access to mental health professionals, whether through an Employee

Assistance Program (EAP) or other means, ensures that support is available when needed.

The project manager's own mental health should not be neglected. Engaging in regular self-care practices, such as exercise, meditation, or hobbies, can help maintain a healthy work-life balance. It is also important for project managers to seek support when necessary, whether through professional counseling or peer support groups. By prioritizing their own wellbeing, project managers set a positive example for their team.

In the high-stakes world of project management, promoting mental health and wellbeing is not just a nicety but a necessity. A mentally healthy team is more resilient, creative, and productive, better equipped to handle the inevitable challenges that arise. By fostering a supportive environment, maintaining clear boundaries, and providing the necessary resources, project managers can ensure that their team remains strong and motivated, even in the face of adversity.

Creating a Resilient Team Culture

A project manager's role often involves navigating through challenging terrains, especially when the time comes to deliver bad news. One of the most vital strategies in such situations is fostering a resilient team culture. This subchapter delves into the essence of creating an environment where resilience thrives, enabling the team to handle setbacks without losing momentum.

Imagine a workplace where every team member feels supported, valued, and prepared to face challenges head-on. It starts with trust. Building trust is not an overnight task; it requires consistent, transparent communication and actions that align with words. When team members believe in their leader's integrity, they are more likely to stand together during tough times. Trust acts as the glue that binds the team, making it possible to tackle bad news collectively rather than in isolation.

Empathy plays a crucial role in cultivating resilience. A project manager who understands and acknowledges the emotions and perspectives of their team members can foster a supportive atmosphere. This involves active listening, validating feelings, and showing genuine concern for their well-being. By demonstrating empathy, the project manager can create a safe space where team members feel comfortable expressing their concerns and uncertainties.

Encouraging open communication is another cornerstone of a resilient team culture. When team members are encouraged to voice their opinions, share ideas, and discuss problems without fear of retribution, it creates a sense of ownership and accountability. Regular check-ins, team meetings, and feedback sessions can serve as platforms for such open dialogues. This transparency helps in identifying potential issues early and collaboratively finding solutions, thereby minimizing the impact of bad news when it arises.

Fostering a growth mindset within the team can transform challenges into learning opportunities. When setbacks are viewed not as failures but as chances to improve and innovate, the team becomes more adaptable and resilient. Project managers can promote this mindset by celebrating small wins, acknowledging efforts, and framing mistakes as part of the learning curve. Providing opportunities for professional development and continuous learning also reinforces this culture.

Recognition and appreciation are powerful motivators. Acknowledging the hard work and achievements of team members, even in the face of adversity, boosts morale and reinforces their commitment to the project. Simple gestures such as verbal praise, written acknowledgments, or team celebrations can go a long way in maintaining a positive atmosphere. When team members feel valued and appreciated, they are more likely to stay motivated and resilient.

Another crucial aspect is fostering a sense of community and support within the team. Encouraging collaboration rather than competition helps build strong interpersonal relationships. Team-building activities, both formal and informal, can strengthen bonds and create a sense of camaraderie. When team members feel connected and supportive of each other, they are better equipped to handle collective challenges.

A resilient team culture also involves preparing for the unexpected. This includes having contingency plans, conducting risk assessments, and ensuring that the team is well-equipped to handle crises. Training sessions on stress management, problem-solving, and adaptability can further enhance the team's ability to navigate through difficult times.

In essence, creating a resilient team culture is about laying a strong foundation of trust, empathy, open communication, growth mindset, recognition, community, and preparedness. With these elements in place, a project manager can deliver bad news in a manner that the team can absorb, process, and bounce back from, stronger and more united than before.

Navigating Future Challenges

The landscape of project management is dynamic, constantly evolving with new methodologies, technologies, and expectations. Project managers often find themselves at the intersection of these changes, tasked with not only steering their teams through complex projects but also delivering difficult news when things don't go as planned. As we look ahead, it's crucial to understand how to navigate future challenges and effectively communicate setbacks.

One of the most significant challenges on the horizon is the rapid pace of technological advancement. Artificial intelligence, machine learning, and automation are becoming integral to project management. While these technologies can enhance efficiency and decision-making, they also introduce new complexities. Project managers must be adept at understanding these tools and their implications. When a project encounters issues related to technology, explaining these problems to stakeholders who may not have a technical background becomes a delicate task. Clear, concise communication is essential, ensuring that the impact and potential solutions are well understood.

Globalization adds another layer of complexity. Projects often involve teams spread across different time zones and cultures. This diversity can lead to misunderstandings and miscommunications. When delivering bad news, project managers must be culturally sensitive and aware of how different stakeholders might perceive and react to the information. A one-size-fits-all approach is rarely effective in a global context. Tailoring the message to resonate with each audience segment is crucial.

The increasing emphasis on sustainability and social responsibility is reshaping project priorities. Stakeholders are more concerned than ever about the environmental and social impact of projects. When setbacks occur, especially those affecting these areas, project managers need to address stakeholders' concerns transparently. Providing a balanced view of the situation, including both the challenges and the steps being taken to mitigate negative impacts, can help maintain trust and credibility.

Economic fluctuations and market uncertainties also pose significant challenges. Projects are often at the mercy of external economic conditions, which can lead to budget cuts, resource constraints, or shifting priorities. Communicating these changes and their repercussions requires a nuanced approach. Project managers must provide a realistic assessment of the situation while also offering a path forward. It's essential to manage expectations carefully, balancing optimism with pragmatism.

Human factors remain a constant challenge. Team dynamics, morale, and individual performance can all impact a project's trajectory. When issues arise, such as a key team member leaving or internal conflicts disrupting progress, project managers must address these problems head-on. Delivering bad news in these scenarios requires empathy and a focus on solutions. Acknowledging the human element and showing genuine concern for the team can help in navigating these challenges more smoothly.

The future of project management will undoubtedly bring new challenges, but the core principles of effective communication and leadership remain the same. Project managers must stay adaptable, continuously updating their skills and strategies to meet the demands of an ever-changing landscape. By fostering an environment of transparency and trust, they can navigate even the most difficult situations with confidence and poise.

Chapter 9: Case Studies and Real-Life Examples

Successful Strategies in Action

In the realm of project management, delivering bad news is an inevitable task that requires skill, empathy, and strategic finesse. Successful project managers understand that the way negative updates are communicated can significantly impact team morale, stakeholder trust, and the project's overall trajectory. To navigate these challenging conversations, seasoned professionals employ a variety of effective strategies that not only convey the necessary information but also foster a constructive atmosphere.

One of the most effective strategies is to prepare thoroughly before delivering the news. This involves gathering all pertinent facts and figures, understanding the root cause of the issue, and anticipating potential questions from the audience. Armed with a comprehensive understanding of the situation, the project manager can present a clear and concise narrative that minimizes confusion and speculation. Preparation also includes considering the emotional impact on the recipients and planning how to address their concerns empathetically.

Choosing the right time and setting for the conversation is another critical aspect. Project managers often opt for face-to-face meetings or video calls to ensure a personal touch, allowing for immediate feedback and emotional support. Ensuring privacy and a distraction-free environment helps create a space where individuals feel comfortable expressing their thoughts and feelings. Timing the delivery to avoid high-stress moments, such as right before a major deadline, can also help mitigate the emotional blow.

Clarity and honesty are paramount when conveying bad news. Successful project managers avoid sugarcoating the situation or downplaying its severity. Instead, they present the facts straightforwardly, ensuring that all stakeholders have a clear understanding of the issue at hand. Honesty fosters trust and credibility, even in difficult times. Alongside the facts, providing a well-thought-out plan for addressing the problem demonstrates proactive leadership and reassures stakeholders that there is a path forward.

Empathy plays a crucial role in these conversations. Acknowledging the emotions and concerns of the team and stakeholders helps in building a supportive environment. Project managers often express their understanding of the disappointment or frustration that the news may cause, validating the feelings of those affected. This emotional intelligence not only strengthens relationships but also encourages open dialogue and collaborative problem-solving.

Another key strategy is to frame the bad news within the broader context of the project's goals and vision. By linking the current setback to the overall objectives, project managers can help stakeholders see the bigger picture and maintain their commitment to the project's success. This approach also provides an opportunity to highlight any positive aspects, such as lessons learned or opportunities for improvement, which can shift the focus from the problem to potential solutions.

Communication does not end with the initial delivery of bad news. Successful project managers follow up with regular updates on the progress of the corrective actions and remain available for further discussions. This ongoing dialogue ensures transparency and keeps the lines of communication open, allowing for continuous feedback and adjustments as needed.

Through meticulous preparation, strategic timing, clear and honest communication, empathetic engagement, and contextual framing, project managers can effectively navigate the challenging task of delivering bad news. These strategies not only help in managing immediate reactions but also contribute to building a resilient and cohesive team capable of overcoming obstacles and achieving long-term success.

Lessons from Failures

Navigating the turbulent waters of project management often involves facing setbacks and obstacles. These moments, though challenging, present invaluable opportunities for growth and learning. When delivering bad news, a project manager must harness the lessons gleaned from past failures to effectively communicate and steer the team through adversity.

Imagine a project that has veered off course, deadlines missed, and budgets exceeded. The immediate response might be to find someone to blame or to cover up the shortfall. However, a seasoned project manager understands that transparency and accountability are paramount. Acknowledging the missteps and openly discussing what went wrong fosters a culture of trust and continuous improvement.

One critical lesson from past failures is the importance of clear and consistent communication. Ambiguity can lead to misunderstandings and further complications. By providing precise updates and outlining the issues candidly, a project manager can prevent misinformation and speculation. This approach not only keeps stakeholders informed but also demonstrates a commitment to transparency and integrity.

Another key takeaway is the need for thorough risk management. Many project pitfalls stem from unforeseen risks that were not adequately planned for. By reflecting on past projects where risks materialized unexpectedly, a project manager can develop more robust risk assessment strategies. This involves identifying potential risks early, evaluating their impact, and establishing contingency plans. When bad news arises, having a well-thought-out risk management plan allows for a more structured and less reactive response.

Understanding the root cause of failures is also crucial. Superficial solutions may offer temporary relief but fail to address underlying issues. A project manager should delve deep into the causes of setbacks, whether they stem from resource shortages, unrealistic timelines, or misaligned expectations. By conducting thorough post-mortem analyses and learning from these insights, future projects can be better safeguarded against similar pitfalls.

Empathy and emotional intelligence play significant roles when conveying bad news. Recognizing the emotional impact on the team and stakeholders is essential. A project manager should approach such situations with sensitivity, acknowledging the efforts of the team and the disappointment that accompanies setbacks. This empathetic approach helps in maintaining morale and fostering a supportive environment.

Another lesson is the value of adaptability. Projects rarely go exactly as planned, and the ability to pivot and adjust course is vital. Learning from past failures involves understanding when to change strategies and being open to innovative solutions. This flexibility can turn potential failures into opportunities for creative problem-solving and resilience.

Documentation and knowledge sharing are also pivotal. Capturing the lessons learned from failures in a structured format ensures that the knowledge is accessible for future projects. This practice not only aids in preventing repeat mistakes but also contributes to a culture of continuous learning within the organization.

Lastly, fostering a culture where failure is viewed as a learning opportunity rather than a setback encourages experimentation and innovation. When team members feel safe to take calculated risks without fear of retribution, they are more likely to contribute creative solutions and drive the project forward.

In essence, the experiences of past failures equip a project manager with the insights and strategies needed to handle bad news with grace and effectiveness. By embracing transparency, thorough risk management, empathetic communication, adaptability, and a culture of learning, a project manager can transform setbacks into stepping stones for future success.

Industry-Specific Scenarios

In the bustling world of healthcare, project managers often find themselves navigating a labyrinth of regulations, patient expectations, and technological advancements. Imagine a scenario where a critical hospital project, such as the installation of a new electronic health record (EHR) system, faces unexpected delays. The ripple effects are vast, impacting doctors, nurses, and ultimately, patient care. A project manager in this setting must deliver the news with a blend of empathy and precision. They must prepare a comprehensive report detailing the reasons for the delay, potential impacts on patient care, and a revised timeline. Additionally, they must collaborate closely with medical staff to ensure that temporary measures are in place to maintain patient safety and data integrity.

In the fast-paced tech industry, where innovation is the cornerstone of success, project delays can mean lost market opportunities and a tarnished reputation. Consider a project manager at a software development firm who must inform stakeholders that a highly anticipated app launch will be postponed due to unforeseen technical challenges. Here, the project manager needs to communicate the news with a focus on transparency and solutions. They might organize a virtual meeting, presenting a detailed analysis of the issues encountered, the steps being taken to address them, and a realistic new launch date. By providing a clear action plan and demonstrating a commitment to quality, the project manager can maintain stakeholder confidence and mitigate potential fallout.

In the construction industry, delays and cost overruns are not uncommon, but they can have significant financial implications. Picture a project manager overseeing the construction of a new commercial building who must inform the client that the project will exceed the budget due to unexpected ground conditions. This news requires a delicate balance of honesty and reassurance. The project manager should prepare a detailed report, including the specific reasons for the cost overrun, the projected additional expenses, and any possible cost-saving measures. A face-to-face meeting with the client, accompanied by visual aids such as charts and diagrams, can help convey the information clearly and foster a collaborative approach to finding solutions.

In the world of finance, project delays can affect market predictions, investment strategies, and client trust. Consider a project manager at an investment firm who needs to inform clients that a new financial product launch will be delayed due to regulatory compliance issues. The communication strategy here must emphasize the importance of adherence to regulations and the long-term benefits of ensuring compliance. The project manager should provide a detailed explanation of the regulatory challenges, the steps being taken to resolve them, and the revised timeline for the product launch. By highlighting the firm's dedication to ethical practices and client protection, the project manager can reassure clients and maintain their trust.

In the entertainment industry, where timing can be crucial for the success of a project, delays can be particularly challenging. Imagine a project manager working on a major film production who must inform the studio executives that the film's release date will be pushed back due to post-production issues. The project manager needs to communicate this news with a focus on the creative and technical aspects of the delay. They should present a detailed report outlining the specific post-production challenges, the measures being taken to address them, and a revised release schedule. By emphasizing the commitment to delivering a high-quality final product, the project manager can help the studio understand the necessity of the delay and maintain their support.

Each industry presents unique challenges and requires tailored communication strategies to deliver bad news effectively. By understanding the specific context and needs of their industry, project managers can navigate these difficult conversations with professionalism and empathy, ensuring that stakeholders remain informed and engaged throughout the project lifecycle.

Adapting Techniques to Different Contexts

Project management entails navigating a complex landscape filled with various challenges, and one of the most daunting tasks is delivering bad news. Effective communication, especially when conveying unfavorable updates, is crucial for maintaining trust, morale, and project momentum. The strategies for delivering bad news must be tailored to fit the specific context, as different situations demand different approaches. Recognizing the unique nuances of each context can significantly enhance the effectiveness of the communication process.

In a corporate setting, the hierarchical structure and formal atmosphere necessitate a more structured approach. When addressing senior management, a project manager must prioritize clarity and conciseness. Presenting the bad news in a straightforward manner, supported by data and a clear action plan, helps in mitigating the impact. For instance, if a project is facing delays, it is essential to outline the reasons, the steps being taken to address the issue, and the revised timeline. This approach demonstrates accountability and proactivity, which are highly valued in a corporate environment.

Conversely, when dealing with a team of developers or engineers, a more collaborative approach may be more effective.

Technical teams often appreciate transparency and detailed explanations. Engaging the team in a problem-solving discussion not only helps in finding a solution but also fosters a sense of ownership and collective responsibility. For example, if a critical component of a project has failed, discussing the technical challenges and potential solutions openly can lead to innovative ideas and stronger team cohesion.

In client-facing scenarios, the project manager must balance honesty with diplomacy. Clients invest resources and trust in a project, so delivering bad news requires a tactful approach that reassures them of the project's viability. It is important to communicate the issue clearly, explain its impact on the project, and provide a well-thought-out plan to address it. Additionally, showing empathy and understanding the client's perspective can help in maintaining a positive relationship. For example, if budget constraints are causing project setbacks, discussing alternative solutions and potential compromises can help in finding a mutually agreeable path forward.

Non-profit organizations often operate under different constraints and expectations compared to corporate environments. Here, the focus might be on the broader mission and the impact on the community. When delivering bad news, it is crucial to connect the issue to the organization's values and goals. Explaining how the problem affects the overall mission and proposing solutions that align with the organization's objectives can garner support and understanding. For instance, if a funding shortfall threatens a project, highlighting the importance of the project and exploring alternative funding options can help in rallying support from stakeholders.

Remote work settings present unique challenges for delivering bad news, primarily due to the lack of face-to-face interaction. In such contexts, the project manager must leverage technology to ensure clear and effective communication. Video calls can provide a more personal touch than emails or instant messages. It is also important to be mindful of time zones and cultural differences when scheduling and conducting these communications. Ensuring that everyone has the opportunity to ask questions and express concerns can help in addressing any misunderstandings and fostering a collaborative environment.

Tailoring communication techniques to the specific context not only helps in delivering bad news more effectively but also strengthens the overall project management process. By understanding and adapting to the unique characteristics of each situation, a project manager can navigate the complexities of bad news delivery with greater skill and sensitivity.

Chapter 10: Ethics and Professionalism

Maintaining Integrity

A project manager's role is often a balancing act between various stakeholders, deadlines, and deliverables. Among the many responsibilities, delivering bad news is one of the most challenging tasks. It requires not just tact but also an unwavering commitment to honesty and ethical behavior. The essence of maintaining integrity lies at the heart of this daunting task.

At the outset, integrity demands transparency. When a project hits a snag, whether it be a delay, budget overrun, or a critical error, the project manager must resist the urge to sugarcoat the situation. Transparency involves presenting the facts as they are, without distortion. This approach builds trust with stakeholders, as they are more likely to appreciate the honesty rather than feel misled by half-truths or omissions.

The next facet of integrity is accountability. A project manager must own the situation, regardless of whether the fault lies with them or external factors. This means acknowledging the problem, understanding its root causes, and communicating this effectively to all concerned parties. Accountability also extends to outlining the steps being taken to address the issue. By demonstrating a proactive stance, the project manager reassures stakeholders that the situation is under control and that efforts are being made to rectify it.

Another critical element is consistency. Consistency in communication and actions reinforces the credibility of the project manager. When bad news is delivered, it should be done in a manner consistent with previous communications and aligned with the established norms and expectations of the organization. This consistency helps to mitigate the shock and maintains a level of predictability, which can be comforting to stakeholders.

Empathy plays a significant role in maintaining integrity while delivering bad news. Understanding the impact of the news on various stakeholders and addressing their concerns with genuine care can make a substantial difference. Empathy involves not just acknowledging their feelings but also offering support and solutions to help them navigate the challenges posed by the bad news. This human touch fosters a sense of solidarity and shared purpose.

Moreover, integrity involves a commitment to ethical behavior. This means avoiding the temptation to shift blame or manipulate the situation to one's advantage. Ethical behavior ensures that the project manager remains focused on the collective good rather than individual gain. This ethical stance resonates with stakeholders, reinforcing their trust in the project manager's leadership.

Communication skills are paramount in maintaining integrity. The ability to convey bad news clearly, concisely, and respectfully is an art that every project manager must master. This involves choosing the right moment, the right medium, and the right words. Effective communication ensures that the message is received and understood without unnecessary confusion or misinterpretation.

In the realm of project management, maintaining integrity while delivering bad news is not just about adhering to moral principles; it is about fostering a culture of trust, accountability, and respect. It is about standing firm in the face of adversity and leading with honesty and empathy. While the task may be daunting, the rewards of maintaining integrity are profound, paving the way for stronger relationships and more resilient projects.

Balancing Transparency with Sensitivity

Navigating the delicate balance between transparency and sensitivity is a crucial skill for any project manager tasked with delivering bad news. It involves the fine art of being honest and forthcoming while also being considerate of the emotions and responses of the stakeholders involved. This balance ensures that the integrity of the information is maintained without causing unnecessary distress or panic.

When faced with the need to communicate unfavorable updates, the project manager must first assess the nature and impact of the news. Understanding the full scope of the situation allows for a more strategic approach in delivering the message. It is essential to gather all relevant facts, anticipate potential questions, and prepare clear, concise responses. This preparation not only demonstrates professionalism but also helps in managing the conversation more effectively.

The next step involves selecting the appropriate medium for communication. While emails or written reports may suffice for minor issues, more significant or sensitive matters often require face-to-face meetings or video conferences. These methods provide a more personal touch, allowing the project manager to convey empathy and gauge the immediate reactions of the stakeholders. In-person or virtual meetings also facilitate a two-way dialogue, enabling stakeholders to voice their concerns and ask questions in real-time.

During the delivery of the bad news, the project manager should aim for a tone that is both straightforward and compassionate. It is important to be direct about the issue at hand without sugarcoating or downplaying its significance. However, this directness should be tempered with empathy, acknowledging the potential impact on the stakeholders and expressing genuine concern for their feelings. Phrases such as "I understand this is disappointing" or "I recognize the challenges this presents" can help in conveying sensitivity.

In addition to the tone, the structure of the message plays a vital role. Starting with a brief overview of the situation, followed by a detailed explanation of the issue, and concluding with the steps being taken to address it, provides a clear and logical flow of information. This approach helps in maintaining transparency while also offering reassurance that proactive measures are being implemented to mitigate the problem.

Listening is another critical component in balancing transparency with sensitivity. After delivering the news, the project manager should give ample time for stakeholders to process the information and express their reactions. Active listening, characterized by maintaining eye contact, nodding, and paraphrasing their concerns, demonstrates respect and validates their feelings. It also provides valuable insights into their perspectives, which can inform future communications and decision-making processes.

Providing support and resources is equally important. Offering solutions, alternatives, or additional assistance not only addresses the immediate issue but also shows a commitment to the well-being of the stakeholders. This proactive stance can help in rebuilding trust and confidence, which may have been shaken by the bad news.

Ultimately, the goal is to foster an environment where honesty and compassion coexist. By being transparent about the challenges while also being sensitive to the emotional landscape, the project manager can navigate the complexities of delivering bad news with integrity and care. This balanced approach not only preserves the trust and respect of the stakeholders but also reinforces the project manager's credibility and leadership.

Confidentiality Concerns

In the intricate web of project management, confidentiality concerns hold significant weight, particularly when delivering bad news. The project manager must navigate this delicate landscape with a keen awareness of the sensitive nature of the information. Safeguarding confidentiality is not just a matter of professionalism; it is a fundamental aspect of maintaining trust and integrity within the team and with stakeholders.

Imagine a scenario where a project is facing significant delays due to unforeseen technical issues. The project manager is aware that divulging too much information too soon could incite unnecessary panic or speculation. It is crucial to carefully consider who needs to know what, and when they need to know it. The project manager must strike a balance between transparency and discretion.

When delivering bad news, the project manager must ensure that the information is shared with the appropriate parties. This often involves a tiered approach, where different levels of detail are provided to different stakeholders based on their role and need to know. For instance, the core project team may need a comprehensive understanding of the technical challenges, while senior executives may only require a high-level overview of the impact on timelines and budget.

The method of communication also plays a pivotal role in maintaining confidentiality. One-on-one meetings or small group discussions are often more effective than mass emails or public announcements. This approach not only helps control the dissemination of information but also allows for a more personalized and empathetic delivery. The project manager can gauge reactions and address concerns in real-time, fostering a sense of trust and collaboration.

Furthermore, documentation practices must be meticulously managed. Sensitive information should be clearly marked and access restricted to those who genuinely need it. Digital tools and platforms used for project management should have robust security features to protect confidential data. The project manager must be vigilant about who has access to various documents and ensure that permissions are regularly reviewed and updated.

Another critical aspect is the timing of the communication. Prematurely sharing bad news can lead to unnecessary stress and distraction, while delaying too long can erode trust and exacerbate the issue. The project manager must carefully plan the timing, ensuring that stakeholders are informed promptly but also thoughtfully. This often requires a deep understanding of the project's dynamics and the stakeholders' expectations and sensitivities.

Confidentiality concerns also extend to the language used. The project manager must be mindful of how the information is framed. Clear, concise, and neutral language helps prevent misinterpretation and rumor-mongering. It is essential to avoid jargon or technical terms that may confuse or alarm stakeholders. Instead, the focus should be on delivering a coherent message that is easy to understand and digest.

In dealing with confidentiality concerns, the project manager must also be prepared for follow-up questions and discussions. Providing a clear pathway for feedback and queries helps manage the flow of information and ensures that stakeholders feel heard and supported. This ongoing communication loop is vital for maintaining trust and mitigating the impact of the bad news.

Ultimately, handling confidentiality concerns when delivering bad news is a nuanced and multifaceted challenge. It requires a blend of strategic thinking, emotional intelligence, and meticulous planning. By carefully managing who, how, and when information is shared, the project manager can uphold the principles of confidentiality while navigating the complexities of delivering difficult news.

Ethical Decision-Making Frameworks

Navigating the complexities of delivering bad news in a project management context requires not only sensitivity and tact but also a strong ethical foundation. Ethical decision-making frameworks serve as valuable guides to ensure that project managers act with integrity and accountability. These frameworks provide structured approaches to making decisions that are not only legally compliant but also morally sound.

One widely recognized framework is the Utilitarian Approach, which emphasizes the greatest good for the greatest number. When faced with the task of delivering bad news, a project manager might evaluate the potential outcomes of various communication strategies and choose the one that minimizes harm while maximizing overall benefit. For instance, if a project delay affects multiple stakeholders, the manager might decide to communicate the delay early and transparently to allow all parties to adjust their plans accordingly. This approach ensures that the decision is made in consideration of the broader impact on all stakeholders involved.

Another essential framework is the Rights Approach, which focuses on respecting and protecting the individual rights of all parties. This framework is particularly relevant when dealing with sensitive information or when the bad news has significant personal implications for team members or stakeholders. A project manager adhering to the Rights Approach would ensure that the information is communicated privately and respectfully, safeguarding the dignity and privacy of those affected. This might involve one-on-one meetings or confidential communications to deliver the news in a manner that honors the rights of the individuals involved.

The Fairness or Justice Approach is another critical ethical framework. It emphasizes fairness, equity, and impartiality in decision-making. When delivering bad news, a project manager guided by this approach would strive to ensure that the communication and any subsequent actions do not favor one party over another unjustly. For example, if budget cuts necessitate reducing project scope, the manager would transparently explain the criteria used to make those reductions, ensuring that the process is perceived as fair and unbiased by all team members and stakeholders.

The Common Good Approach underscores the importance of community and the welfare of the broader group. In a project setting, this might mean considering how the bad news and its delivery will affect the team's morale, cohesion, and long-term success. A project manager might choose to frame the bad news within the context of the project's overall goals and the collective benefit, fostering a sense of shared purpose and mutual support. This approach helps to maintain a positive and collaborative team environment even in the face of setbacks.

Lastly, the Virtue Approach focuses on the character and virtues of the decision-maker. Project managers who adopt this framework would reflect on the virtues they wish to embody, such as honesty, courage, empathy, and responsibility. Delivering bad news with these virtues in mind means being honest about the situation, courageous in facing the consequences, empathetic towards those affected, and responsible for finding solutions and mitigating negative impacts. This approach not only guides the immediate action but also shapes the manager's reputation and the trust others place in their leadership.

Incorporating these ethical decision-making frameworks into the process of delivering bad news helps project managers navigate these challenging situations with integrity and respect. By doing so, they not only address the immediate issue at hand but also contribute to a culture of ethical behavior and trust within their teams and organizations.

Chapter 11: Tools and Resources

Communication Platforms

Effective communication is the cornerstone of successful project management, especially when it comes to delivering bad news. In today's digital age, project managers have an array of communication platforms at their disposal, each with its own strengths and weaknesses. Understanding these platforms is crucial for determining the most appropriate medium for conveying difficult messages.

Email remains one of the most commonly used communication tools in the professional world. Its asynchronous nature allows recipients to process the information at their own pace, which can be beneficial when delivering bad news. However, the lack of immediate feedback and the potential for misinterpretation make it less ideal for sensitive information. Tone and intent can easily be misconstrued, leading to further complications. Therefore, while email can be useful for documenting conversations and providing detailed explanations, it should be used cautiously for delivering particularly distressing news.

Video conferencing has gained significant traction, especially with the rise of remote work. Platforms like Zoom, Microsoft

Teams, and Google Meet offer the advantage of face-to-face interaction, even when team members are geographically dispersed. The visual and auditory cues available in video calls can help in conveying empathy and sincerity, which are essential when delivering bad news. The ability to see the recipient's reactions in real-time allows for immediate clarification and support, making it easier to manage the emotional impact. However, technical issues such as poor internet connection can sometimes disrupt the flow of communication.

Instant messaging platforms like Slack, Microsoft Teams, and WhatsApp offer a more informal and immediate way to communicate. They are excellent for quick updates and clarifications but may not be suitable for delivering bad news due to their casual nature. The brevity required in instant messaging can lead to oversimplification of complex issues, increasing the risk of misunderstanding. Additionally, the lack of non-verbal cues can make it difficult to convey the appropriate level of empathy and concern. Instant messaging should be reserved for follow-up discussions rather than the initial delivery of bad news.

Telephone calls provide a more personal touch compared to email and instant messaging. The tone of voice can convey empathy and seriousness, helping to mitigate the negative impact of the news. While not as rich in non-verbal cues as video conferencing, phone calls allow for immediate feedback and clarification. They are particularly useful when a quick response is needed or when the recipient may not have access to video conferencing tools. However, the lack of visual interaction can sometimes make it challenging to fully gauge the recipient's emotional state.

Face-to-face meetings are often considered the gold standard for delivering bad news. The ability to observe body language and facial expressions provides a comprehensive understanding of the recipient's reaction. This allows for a more nuanced and empathetic approach, making it easier to offer immediate support and reassurance. Face-to-face interactions also facilitate a more open and honest dialogue, which can be crucial for resolving any issues that may arise from the bad news. However, logistical challenges and time constraints can make this option less feasible, especially in large or geographically dispersed teams.

Each communication platform has its own set of advantages and limitations. The choice of platform should be guided by the nature of the bad news, the relationship with the recipient, and the context in which the communication is taking place. By carefully selecting the appropriate medium, project managers can deliver bad news in a manner that is respectful, empathetic, and effective.

Project Management Software

In the modern landscape of project management, software tools have become indispensable allies. These digital platforms streamline workflows, enhance communication, and provide invaluable insights into project progress. For a project manager, especially one tasked with delivering unwelcome news, the right software can be a crucial asset.

Imagine having a centralized hub where every detail of the project is meticulously documented. Project management software offers this capability, allowing managers to track tasks, deadlines, and resource allocation with pinpoint accuracy. This level of organization helps ensure that when setbacks occur, the root causes are easily identifiable. Detailed logs and reports generated by these tools can provide a clear narrative, making it easier to explain why certain decisions were made and what led to the current situation.

Communication is another critical area where project management software shines. Within these platforms, team members can collaborate in real-time, sharing updates, documents, and feedback instantaneously. This fosters a transparent environment where everyone is kept in the loop, reducing the likelihood of misunderstandings. When it comes time to deliver bad news, having a history of transparent communication can build trust and credibility. Stakeholders are more likely to respond positively if they feel they have been kept informed throughout the project.

Moreover, these tools often come with built-in analytics and reporting features. By leveraging these capabilities, a project manager can present data-driven insights when delivering bad news. Instead of relying on subjective explanations, they can offer concrete evidence to support their points. Charts, graphs, and performance metrics can illustrate the challenges faced and the steps taken to mitigate them. This objective approach can help in managing expectations and demonstrating that despite the setbacks, the project has been handled with professionalism and diligence.

Risk management is another domain where project management software proves its worth. These platforms often include risk assessment modules that help identify potential issues before they become critical. By regularly updating the risk register and monitoring key indicators, a project manager can proactively address concerns. If a risk does materialize into a problem, the pre-planned mitigation strategies can be swiftly implemented. This preparedness can soften the blow of bad news, showing that the team was not caught off guard and had considered various contingencies.

Resource management is equally enhanced by these tools. Allocating and reallocating resources becomes a more informed process, guided by the data captured within the software. When bad news involves delays or budget overruns, a project manager can show a detailed account of resource utilization. This transparency can help justify decisions and provide a roadmap for corrective actions.

Furthermore, project management software often includes features for stakeholder management. These tools allow for the categorization and prioritization of stakeholders, ensuring that communication is tailored to the needs of each group. When delivering bad news, this targeted approach can make a significant difference. By addressing the specific concerns of each stakeholder, a project manager can foster a more supportive and understanding environment.

In essence, project management software serves as a multifaceted tool that enhances every aspect of project delivery. For a project manager facing the daunting task of delivering bad news, these platforms offer the structure, transparency, and analytical power needed to handle the situation with grace and competence.

Training and Development Programs

Cultivating the ability to deliver bad news effectively is a skill that can be honed through dedicated training and development programs. Project managers often find themselves in situations where they must communicate disappointing updates to stakeholders, team members, or clients. The foundation for managing these challenging conversations lies in a well-structured training regime that focuses on both the technical aspects of project management and the subtleties of human interaction.

Training programs often start with the basics of effective communication. Understanding the principles of clear, concise, and empathetic communication is crucial. Techniques such as active listening, non-verbal cues, and emotional intelligence are emphasized. These elements are essential in ensuring that the message is not only delivered but also received in the right spirit. Role-playing exercises are commonly used to simulate real-life scenarios, allowing project managers to practice delivering bad news in a controlled environment. This experiential learning helps in building confidence and improving the ability to handle such situations with grace and professionalism.

Another critical component of these training programs is conflict resolution. Bad news often leads to conflict, either overt or subtle, and project managers must be equipped to navigate these turbulent waters. Training sessions focus on strategies to de-escalate tension, mediate disagreements, and find mutually acceptable solutions. Understanding the root causes of conflict and addressing them proactively can prevent situations from escalating and help maintain a positive team dynamic.

Emphasis is also placed on cultural sensitivity and adaptability. In today's globalized work environment, project managers often work with diverse teams across different geographical locations. Training programs incorporate modules on cultural awareness, helping managers understand and respect cultural differences in communication styles, expectations, and reactions to bad news. This knowledge is vital in crafting messages that are considerate of the recipient's cultural context, thereby reducing the risk of misunderstandings and fostering a more inclusive work environment.

Emotional resilience is another area of focus. Delivering bad news can be emotionally taxing, and project managers must develop the resilience to handle the stress associated with these tasks. Training programs include techniques for managing stress, maintaining a positive outlook, and developing a support network. Mindfulness exercises, stress management workshops, and peer support groups are some of the methods used to build emotional resilience. This aspect of training ensures that project managers remain effective and composed, even in the face of adversity.

Feedback mechanisms are integrated into the training programs to provide continuous improvement. Constructive feedback from trainers and peers helps project managers refine their communication skills and strategies. Regular assessments and follow-up sessions ensure that the learning is reinforced and adapted to real-world scenarios. This iterative process of learning and feedback fosters a culture of continuous improvement, enabling project managers to become more adept at handling difficult conversations over time.

Moreover, these programs often include mentorship opportunities, where experienced project managers share their insights and strategies for delivering bad news. Mentorship provides a valuable perspective, offering practical advice and support based on real-world experiences. This exchange of knowledge not only enriches the learning experience but also builds a sense of community and shared purpose among project managers.

Through comprehensive training and development programs, project managers can transform the daunting task of delivering bad news into an opportunity for growth and learning. By equipping themselves with the right tools and techniques, they can navigate these challenging conversations with confidence and empathy, ultimately fostering a more resilient and cohesive project environment.

External Support Systems

Navigating the turbulent waters of delivering bad news as a project manager often requires more than just personal resilience and tact. The intricate web of external support systems can play a pivotal role in mitigating the impact of unfavorable updates. These support systems extend beyond the immediate project team, encompassing a variety of resources and networks designed to provide assistance, guidance, and reinforcement.

One essential component of external support is the organizational infrastructure itself. Within this framework, various departments and functions can offer critical support. For instance, Human Resources can provide training on effective communication strategies and emotional intelligence, equipping project managers with the tools they need to handle difficult conversations. Legal and compliance teams can offer insights into the ramifications of project setbacks, ensuring that the information is conveyed in a manner that adheres to regulatory requirements and minimizes potential liabilities.

Another layer of support comes from professional networks and industry associations. These groups often host forums, workshops, and conferences where project managers can share experiences and strategies related to delivering bad news.

Engaging with peers facing similar challenges can provide valuable perspectives and innovative solutions. It's within these networks that project managers can find mentors who have navigated similar situations and can offer sage advice grounded in experience.

Consultants and external advisors also constitute a significant support system. These professionals bring an outsider's perspective, which can be invaluable in crafting a message that is both honest and constructive. Their expertise can help in anticipating stakeholder reactions and preparing responses to potential questions or concerns. Engaging a communications consultant, for example, might refine the messaging to ensure clarity and empathy, transforming a potentially damaging disclosure into an opportunity for demonstrating transparency and commitment to resolving issues.

Technology, too, serves as a crucial external support system. Project management software and communication tools can facilitate the dissemination of information in a controlled and systematic manner. These platforms often include features that allow for the tracking of project metrics and the generation of reports, which can be used to provide a data-driven context for the bad news. This approach can help stakeholders understand the situation's scope and the steps being taken to address it.

The role of social support networks cannot be underestimated. Family, friends, and colleagues outside the immediate work environment often provide the emotional backing needed during stressful times. These personal connections offer a respite from the professional pressures, enabling project managers to recharge and gain a fresh perspective. Emotional support from trusted individuals can bolster confidence and resilience, essential traits when faced with the daunting task of delivering unwelcome updates.

Incorporating these external support systems into the strategy for delivering bad news can significantly enhance a project manager's ability to manage the situation effectively. The synergy between organizational resources, professional networks, consultants, technology, and personal support creates a robust framework that not only aids in the immediate task of communication but also contributes to long-term professional growth and resilience. By leveraging these diverse resources, project managers can navigate the complexities of their role with greater assurance and competence.

Chapter 12: The Role of Feedback

Soliciting Feedback Effectively

Gaining insights from team members and stakeholders is crucial when delivering unfavorable news in project management. This process not only provides a broader perspective but also fosters a sense of inclusion and shared responsibility among all parties involved. It begins with creating an environment where individuals feel safe to share their honest opinions without fear of retribution. Establishing trust is the cornerstone of effective feedback solicitation.

The atmosphere should be one where open communication is encouraged, and every team member feels their voice is valued. This can be achieved by consistently practicing active listening, showing empathy, and acknowledging contributions. When people believe their input is genuinely considered, they are more likely to provide meaningful and constructive feedback.

Timing and context play significant roles in soliciting feedback. It's important to choose the right moment to ask for input, preferably when the team is not under immediate pressure or stress. Setting a specific time for feedback sessions, such as during regular meetings or dedicated feedback workshops, can help integrate this practice into the project's routine. This approach ensures that feedback is not an afterthought but a structured part of the project management process.

Clarity in communication is essential. When requesting feedback, be specific about what aspects you need insights on. Vague or broad questions can lead to equally ambiguous responses. Instead, ask targeted questions that address particular areas of concern or interest. For example, instead of asking, "What do you think about the project?" a more effective question might be, "How do you feel about the current project timeline and its feasibility?"

Utilizing diverse feedback methods can cater to different communication styles and preferences within the team. Some individuals may be more comfortable providing feedback in a one-on-one setting, while others might prefer written feedback through surveys or anonymous suggestion boxes. Offering multiple channels for feedback ensures that everyone has the opportunity to contribute in a manner they are comfortable with.

Active listening is a critical skill in this process. When receiving feedback, it's important to listen attentively without interrupting. Show that you are engaged by nodding, maintaining eye contact, and summarizing what the speaker has said to ensure understanding. This not only validates the speaker's input but also demonstrates your commitment to considering their perspective.

Once feedback is received, it's crucial to act on it. Acknowledge the input and communicate any steps that will be taken as a result. If certain suggestions cannot be implemented, explain the reasons why. This transparency helps maintain trust and shows that feedback is not merely collected but also valued and used to inform decisions.

Creating a feedback loop is an ongoing process. Regularly revisiting and reflecting on the feedback helps to continually improve project management practices. Encourage a culture where feedback is seen as a tool for growth rather than criticism. Recognizing and celebrating instances where feedback has led to positive changes can reinforce its importance and motivate continued participation.

Effective feedback solicitation is a dynamic and integral part of managing projects, especially when navigating the complexities of delivering bad news. It empowers team members, fosters a collaborative environment, and leads to better-informed decisions, ultimately enhancing the project's success and the team's cohesion.

Giving Constructive Feedback

The room is quiet, the air thick with anticipation as the project manager prepares to deliver feedback. The task is delicate, requiring a balance between honesty and empathy. The project manager knows that the words chosen today can either build bridges or create chasms. Each syllable carries weight, each pause a moment for reflection.

In the soft glow of the conference room lights, the project manager begins by setting a positive tone. Acknowledging the team's hard work and dedication, the manager ensures that the feedback session starts on a note of appreciation. This initial moment of gratitude is like a warm blanket, providing comfort and opening the door to a more receptive audience.

The project manager then transitions into the core of the discussion. It's essential to be specific and clear, avoiding vague statements that could lead to misunderstandings. Instead of saying, "The project didn't go well," the manager opts for, "The timeline for the last phase was delayed by two weeks, which impacted our delivery schedule." This specificity not only clarifies the issue but also sets the stage for a constructive conversation.

Maintaining eye contact, the project manager conveys sincerity and concern. The tone is calm, devoid of any hint of frustration or disappointment. The aim is to create an environment where the team feels safe to discuss the issues openly. The project manager listens actively, nodding occasionally, showing that every word from the team is valued.

The feedback is structured in a way that it addresses the issue without attacking the person. "The report lacked some critical data points," is preferred over, "You failed to include the necessary data." This subtle shift in language ensures that the feedback is perceived as a critique of the work, not the individual. It's about guiding, not blaming.

Next, the project manager offers actionable suggestions. It's not enough to point out what went wrong; it's crucial to provide a path forward. "In future reports, let's ensure we include data from all departments," provides a clear, actionable step that the team can follow. This approach transforms criticism into a learning opportunity, fostering growth and improvement.

Throughout the discussion, the project manager checks in with the team, asking for their thoughts and feelings. "How do you think we can avoid this in the future?" or "What support do you need to improve this aspect?" These questions not only involve the team in the problem-solving process but also empower them to take ownership of their growth.

The conversation is rounded off with a reaffirmation of belief in the team's abilities. The project manager highlights past successes and expresses confidence in the team's potential to overcome the current challenges. This reinforcement builds morale and motivates the team to strive for better results.

As the session concludes, there's a sense of relief and renewed determination in the room. The project manager has not just delivered bad news but has done so in a way that is constructive, supportive, and forward-looking. The team leaves the room not with a sense of failure, but with a clear understanding of their path to improvement and the unwavering support of their leader.

Incorporating Feedback into Practice

Listening attentively to feedback is an essential skill for any project manager, particularly when tasked with delivering bad news. The ability to understand and interpret feedback from stakeholders can significantly influence the outcome of a challenging situation. Constructive feedback serves as a guiding compass, helping to navigate through the complexities of project management and ensuring that the project stays on course despite any obstacles.

The first step in incorporating feedback into practice is to create an environment where open communication is encouraged. This involves establishing trust and demonstrating that all opinions are valued. By fostering a culture of transparency, team members feel more comfortable sharing their thoughts and concerns, which can lead to more productive discussions and innovative solutions.

Once feedback is received, it is crucial to analyze it carefully. This involves distinguishing between constructive criticism and less useful comments. Constructive feedback often comes with specific suggestions for improvement and is delivered in a manner that is intended to help rather than hinder. By focusing on these valuable insights, a project manager can identify areas that need attention and develop strategies to address them.

It is also important to prioritize the feedback based on its relevance and urgency. Not all feedback will be immediately actionable, and some may require more time and resources to implement. By categorizing feedback into short-term and long-term actions, a project manager can create a structured plan to address the most pressing issues first while keeping an eye on future improvements.

After prioritizing, the next step is to integrate the feedback into the project plan. This may involve revising timelines, reallocating resources, or adjusting project goals. Communicating these changes effectively to the team and stakeholders is vital to ensure everyone is aligned and understands the reasons behind the adjustments. Clear communication helps to manage expectations and reduces the risk of further misunderstandings or disappointments.

Monitoring the impact of the implemented feedback is another critical aspect. Regularly reviewing the progress and outcomes of the changes allows the project manager to assess whether the feedback has been effectively incorporated and if it is yielding the desired results. This ongoing evaluation helps to fine-tune the approach and make any necessary adjustments promptly.

Documenting the feedback process and its outcomes is also beneficial. Keeping detailed records of the feedback received, the actions taken, and the results achieved provides valuable insights for future projects. This documentation can serve as a reference point and a learning tool, helping to improve the overall project management process over time.

Engaging the team in reflecting on the feedback process can further enhance its effectiveness. Encouraging team members to share their perspectives on what worked well and what could be improved fosters a culture of continuous improvement. This collective reflection not only strengthens the team's ability to handle similar situations in the future but also builds resilience and adaptability.

Incorporating feedback into practice is an ongoing, iterative process that requires patience, diligence, and a commitment to continuous improvement. By actively listening to stakeholders, analyzing and prioritizing feedback, integrating it into the project plan, and monitoring its impact, a project manager can turn the challenge of delivering bad news into an opportunity for growth and development. Through this approach, feedback becomes a powerful tool that drives the project forward and enhances the overall success of the team.

Continuous Improvement

Within the realm of project management, delivering bad news is an inevitable task that requires not only tact but also a commitment to continuous improvement. This concept is not merely a corporate buzzword, but a vital practice that ensures the sustainability and success of projects. The essence of continuous improvement lies in learning from past experiences, refining processes, and fostering a culture of resilience and adaptability.

One of the fundamental aspects of continuous improvement is the systematic evaluation of project outcomes. After delivering difficult news, it is crucial to conduct a thorough post-mortem analysis. This involves gathering the project team, stakeholders, and any other relevant parties to dissect what went wrong, why it happened, and how it can be prevented in the future. This reflective practice should be approached with an open mind, free from blame, to encourage honest feedback and constructive criticism.

Documentation plays a pivotal role in this process. Detailed records of decisions made, actions taken, and their consequences provide a rich source of data for analysis. By meticulously documenting each step, project managers can identify patterns and trends that may have contributed to the unfavorable outcome. This information becomes invaluable for shaping future strategies and avoiding similar pitfalls.

Training and development are also integral to continuous improvement. A project manager must ensure that their team is equipped with the necessary skills and knowledge to handle challenges effectively. This could involve regular workshops, seminars, and training sessions focused on areas identified as needing improvement. Investing in the professional growth of the team not only enhances their capabilities but also boosts morale and confidence, making them better prepared for future adversities.

Communication is another critical element. Transparent and frequent communication fosters a culture of trust and openness. When bad news is delivered, it should be followed by clear explanations and actionable steps for moving forward. Keeping all stakeholders informed and engaged helps in managing expectations and reduces the potential for misunderstandings. It also provides an opportunity for stakeholders to contribute their insights and suggestions, which can be valuable for refining processes.

Continuous improvement also demands a proactive approach to risk management. Identifying potential risks early and developing contingency plans can mitigate the impact of unforeseen issues. This involves regular risk assessments and updating risk management strategies based on the latest information and lessons learned from past experiences. A proactive stance not only prepares the team for potential challenges but also demonstrates a commitment to excellence and diligence.

Technology can be a powerful ally in the pursuit of continuous improvement. Utilizing project management software and tools can streamline processes, enhance collaboration, and provide real-time data for better decision-making. These technologies can automate routine tasks, freeing up time for the team to focus on more strategic aspects of the project. Additionally, data analytics can offer deeper insights into performance metrics, helping to identify areas for improvement more accurately.

Leadership is the cornerstone of continuous improvement. A project manager must lead by example, demonstrating a commitment to learning and growth. This involves being receptive to feedback, acknowledging mistakes, and showing a willingness to change. By cultivating a positive and progressive mindset, a project manager can inspire their team to strive for excellence and embrace continuous improvement as a core value.

In essence, continuous improvement is about creating a dynamic and responsive project environment. It requires a blend of analytical thinking, effective communication, proactive risk management, and strong leadership. By embedding these principles into the fabric of project management, a project manager can not only navigate the complexities of delivering bad news but also transform challenges into opportunities for growth and success.

Chapter 13: Future Trends in Project Management Communication

Technological Advancements

In the modern landscape of project management, technological advancements play a pivotal role in shaping how information is communicated, including the delivery of bad news. These innovations offer project managers a range of tools and platforms that can facilitate more effective, empathetic, and efficient communication strategies. The evolution of technology has transformed the traditional methods of conveying unwelcome updates, making it possible to handle such delicate tasks with greater precision and sensitivity.

One of the most significant developments in recent years has been the proliferation of project management software. Platforms like Trello, Asana, and Microsoft Project allow managers to track progress, assign tasks, and monitor deadlines in real-time. These tools provide a comprehensive overview of the project's status, enabling managers to identify potential issues early on. When bad news is inevitable, these platforms offer a structured way to present the information, supported by data and analytics that can help stakeholders understand the context and implications.

Video conferencing tools have also revolutionized the way project managers deliver difficult news. Applications like Zoom, Microsoft Teams, and Google Meet offer a more personal touch compared to emails or text messages. The ability to convey tone, facial expressions, and body language can make a significant difference in how the message is received. Video calls provide an opportunity for immediate feedback and discussion, allowing managers to address concerns and answer questions on the spot. This real-time interaction can help mitigate the negative impact of the news and foster a sense of collaboration and support.

The rise of artificial intelligence (AI) and machine learning has introduced new dimensions to project management. Predictive analytics can forecast potential project risks and outcomes, giving managers a heads-up before issues become critical. AI-driven tools can analyze vast amounts of data to identify patterns and trends, offering insights that can inform how bad news is communicated. For instance, sentiment analysis tools can gauge the emotional tone of written communications, helping managers craft messages that are more likely to be received positively.

Moreover, collaboration platforms like Slack and Microsoft Teams have changed the dynamics of team communication. These tools facilitate continuous dialogue among team members, creating an environment of transparency and openness. When bad news needs to be delivered, it can be integrated into the ongoing conversation rather than being a disruptive announcement. This approach can help normalize the occurrence of setbacks and foster a culture where challenges are viewed as opportunities for growth and learning.

Social media and internal communication networks also offer new avenues for delivering updates. Platforms like Yammer or Workplace by Facebook can disseminate information quickly and efficiently to a broad audience. These tools can be particularly useful for large organizations with dispersed teams, ensuring that everyone receives the same message simultaneously. However, the impersonal nature of these platforms necessitates careful consideration of the message's tone and content to avoid misinterpretation or undue alarm.

The advent of these technologies has undeniably enhanced the capacity of project managers to deliver bad news more effectively. However, the human element remains crucial. While technology provides the tools, it is the manager's responsibility to use them thoughtfully and empathetically. Combining technological resources with interpersonal skills can create a balanced approach that not only conveys the necessary information but also supports and motivates the team to navigate through the challenges ahead.

Evolving Team Dynamics

As projects progress, the dynamics within a team can shift in significant and sometimes unexpected ways. Navigating these changes is crucial for a project manager, especially when delivering bad news. The initial stages of a project often see a honeymoon period where enthusiasm is high, and team members are eager to collaborate. However, as challenges emerge and deadlines loom, stress levels can rise, and interpersonal relationships may become strained.

Understanding the intricacies of team dynamics is essential. Team members come from diverse backgrounds and possess varying levels of experience and expertise. These differences can lead to misunderstandings and conflicts, particularly in high-pressure situations. A project manager must be attuned to these shifts and proactively address any signs of discord. Regular check-ins and fostering an open communication environment can help in identifying and mitigating issues early on.

When it comes to delivering bad news, the project manager's approach can significantly influence the team's response and overall morale. Transparency is key. Concealing problems or sugar-coating the truth can lead to a loss of trust, which is difficult to rebuild. Instead, presenting the facts clearly and honestly, while also providing a plan for moving forward, can help maintain the team's confidence and focus.

The method of communication also matters. Choosing the right setting for delivering bad news is crucial. In some cases, a team meeting might be appropriate, allowing for collective discussion and brainstorming solutions. In other instances, one-on-one conversations may be more suitable, particularly if the news impacts individuals differently. Tailoring the approach to the specific situation demonstrates sensitivity and respect for the team's varied needs.

A project manager should also be prepared to manage emotional reactions. Bad news can trigger a range of emotions, from disappointment and frustration to anxiety and anger. Acknowledging these feelings and providing space for team members to express their concerns can help in diffusing tension. Active listening and empathetic responses can go a long way in maintaining a supportive team environment.

Moreover, fostering a culture of resilience and adaptability within the team can make handling bad news more manageable. Encouraging a mindset that views challenges as opportunities for growth rather than setbacks can help in maintaining motivation and morale. Celebrating small wins and progress, even in the face of difficulties, can also contribute to a positive team dynamic.

The project manager's demeanor plays a critical role in setting the tone for the team. Maintaining composure and demonstrating a solution-oriented attitude can inspire confidence. It's important to model the behavior expected from the team, showing that while setbacks are inevitable, they can be overcome with collective effort and a positive outlook.

In essence, evolving team dynamics require continuous attention and adjustment. A project manager must be both a keen observer and an active participant in guiding the team through the ups and downs of a project. By prioritizing clear communication, empathy, and resilience, a project manager can effectively deliver bad news while maintaining a cohesive and motivated team.

Globalization and Communication Challenges

Navigating the intricate web of globalization presents a unique set of challenges for project managers, particularly when it comes to delivering bad news. The interconnected nature of today's global economy means that project teams are often dispersed across various continents, cultures, and time zones. This geographical dispersion necessitates a nuanced approach to communication, demanding sensitivity to cultural differences and an understanding of diverse communication styles.

One of the primary hurdles in this context is the variation in cultural norms and expectations. In some cultures, direct communication is valued, and delivering bad news straightforwardly is seen as a sign of honesty and transparency. In contrast, other cultures may view directness as rude or confrontational, preferring a more indirect approach. A project manager must be adept at reading these cultural cues and tailoring their message accordingly to ensure it is received as intended.

Language barriers also complicate the delivery of unfavorable news. Even when team members are proficient in a common language, nuances, idiomatic expressions, and tone can be easily misinterpreted. This can lead to misunderstandings and exacerbate the negative impact of the news. Therefore, clarity and simplicity in language are paramount. It is often beneficial to follow up verbal communication with written summaries to reinforce the message and provide a reference for team members who may need to process the information at their own pace.

Time zone differences add another layer of complexity. Coordinating a time to deliver bad news when all relevant parties can participate is challenging but necessary. It is crucial to ensure that the timing is considerate of all team members' schedules, avoiding times when individuals may be less receptive, such as late at night or early in the morning. This consideration helps to create an environment where the news can be received and processed with the least amount of additional stress.

Technology plays a vital role in bridging these gaps but is not without its pitfalls. Virtual meetings, emails, and instant messaging are essential tools for global communication, yet they lack the personal touch of face-to-face interactions. Non-verbal cues, which are critical in conveying empathy and understanding, are often lost in digital communication. Project managers must therefore be intentional in their use of technology, perhaps supplementing virtual meetings with video calls to capture more of the human element.

Building a foundation of trust within a global team is essential for effectively delivering bad news. This trust is cultivated through consistent, transparent communication and by demonstrating cultural sensitivity and respect. When team members feel valued and understood, they are more likely to respond constructively to negative information.

In addition to interpersonal communication skills, a project manager should be familiar with the legal and regulatory environments of the countries involved. Different regions have varying regulations regarding employment practices, privacy, and data protection, all of which can influence how bad news should be communicated. Being well-versed in these regulations ensures that the project manager can navigate the complexities of global communication while remaining compliant with local laws.

Effectively managing the challenges of globalization requires a blend of cultural intelligence, linguistic clarity, technological adeptness, and legal awareness. By honing these skills, a project manager can deliver bad news in a manner that is respectful, clear, and conducive to maintaining team cohesion and morale, even in the face of adversity.

Preparing for the Future

Anticipating potential challenges and preparing for future obstacles is an essential skill for any project manager, especially when it comes to delivering bad news. The ability to foresee and plan for difficulties can make the difference between a project that falters and one that ultimately succeeds despite setbacks.

First, cultivating a culture of transparency within the team is paramount. This involves fostering an environment where team members feel comfortable sharing concerns and potential issues without fear of retribution. Regular meetings and open forums can facilitate this openness, allowing problems to be identified and addressed early. A project manager should encourage team members to voice their thoughts and provide a safe space for honest communication.

Developing a robust risk management plan is another critical step. This plan should identify potential risks and outline strategies for mitigating them. By conducting thorough risk assessments, project managers can prioritize which risks need immediate attention and which can be monitored over time. This proactive approach ensures that the team is not caught off guard by unforeseen issues, and it allows for the development of contingency plans.

Scenario planning is a valuable tool in this process. By envisioning various possible futures, project managers can prepare for a range of outcomes. This involves creating detailed scenarios that explore different paths the project might take, considering both best-case and worst-case situations. These scenarios help the team to think through the implications of different events and develop flexible strategies to handle them.

Investing in professional development for both the project manager and the team is also crucial. Continuous learning and improvement can equip the team with the skills they need to handle complex situations. Workshops, training sessions, and certification programs can provide valuable knowledge and techniques for managing projects effectively, even under challenging circumstances.

Building strong relationships with stakeholders is another key aspect of preparing for the future. Establishing trust and open lines of communication with clients, sponsors, and other stakeholders can make it easier to navigate difficult conversations. When stakeholders are kept informed and involved throughout the project, they are more likely to be understanding and supportive when bad news needs to be delivered.

Effective use of technology can also play a significant role. Project management software and tools can help track progress, identify bottlenecks, and predict potential issues before they become critical. These tools can provide real-time data and analytics, allowing project managers to make informed decisions and communicate more effectively with their teams and stakeholders.

Regularly reviewing and updating the project plan is essential to stay on top of changing circumstances. This involves revisiting the project's goals, timelines, and resource allocations to ensure they remain realistic and achievable. By maintaining flexibility and being willing to adjust the plan as needed, project managers can better navigate the complexities of the project lifecycle.

Lastly, maintaining a positive and resilient mindset is vital. Challenges and setbacks are inevitable in any project, but how a project manager responds to them can set the tone for the entire team. Demonstrating calmness, determination, and a solutions-oriented approach can inspire confidence and motivate the team to overcome obstacles together.

By implementing these strategies, project managers can better prepare for the uncertainties of the future, ensuring that they are equipped to deliver bad news in a way that is constructive and minimizes negative impact on the project and its stakeholders.

Chapter 14: Conclusion and Final Thoughts

Summarizing Key Points

The role of a project manager often involves navigating complex terrains, where the delivery of bad news is an inevitable task. This responsibility, although daunting, requires a strategic approach to ensure that the message is conveyed effectively without compromising the integrity of the project or the morale of the team. The essence of delivering bad news lies in the preparation, the manner of communication, and the follow-up actions.

Preparation is the cornerstone of delivering difficult news. A project manager must first understand the nature and implications of the bad news. This involves gathering all relevant facts and assessing the situation thoroughly. By doing so, the manager is equipped with a comprehensive understanding of the issue, which is crucial for addressing any questions or concerns that may arise. Additionally, anticipating the reactions of the stakeholders and preparing appropriate responses can mitigate potential backlash and demonstrate a proactive approach.

The manner in which bad news is communicated is equally important. Transparency and honesty are fundamental principles that should guide this process. While it may be tempting to soften the blow by downplaying the severity of the situation, it is essential to provide a clear and accurate account of the issue. This fosters trust and respect, as stakeholders value honesty over sugar-coated messages. Moreover, the tone and body language used during the delivery play a significant role. A calm, empathetic, and professional demeanor can help in easing the tension and ensuring that the message is received in the intended manner.

Timing is another critical factor. Delivering bad news at an appropriate time can make a significant difference in how it is perceived and handled. Ideally, bad news should be communicated as soon as possible to allow stakeholders ample time to process the information and plan accordingly. Delaying the delivery can lead to speculation, rumors, and a loss of trust, which can further complicate the situation.

The setting in which the news is delivered also matters. A private, comfortable, and neutral environment can help in creating a conducive atmosphere for open and honest communication. This allows stakeholders to express their concerns and emotions without fear of judgment or repercussions. Additionally, choosing the right medium, whether it be a face-to-face meeting, a video call, or a written communication, depends on the nature of the news and the relationship with the stakeholders.

Following the delivery of bad news, it is crucial to focus on the next steps. Providing a clear plan of action and outlining the measures that will be taken to address the issue can instill confidence and demonstrate a commitment to resolving the problem. It is also important to offer support and resources to those affected, showing empathy and understanding of their situation.

Furthermore, maintaining open lines of communication is vital. Regular updates and check-ins can help in managing expectations and keeping stakeholders informed of any progress or changes. This ongoing communication reinforces the message that the project manager is actively engaged in finding solutions and is committed to the success of the project.

In essence, the delivery of bad news by a project manager is a multifaceted process that requires careful preparation, clear and honest communication, appropriate timing and setting, and a focus on actionable solutions. By adhering to these principles, a project manager can navigate this challenging aspect of their role with professionalism and integrity, ultimately contributing to the resilience and success of the project.

Reflecting on Personal Growth

As a project manager, the path to delivering bad news is often fraught with challenges that test both professional skills and personal resilience. The experience of conveying unwelcome updates to stakeholders, team members, or clients can be a crucible for personal growth, revealing strengths and areas for improvement that might have otherwise remained hidden.

Within the crucible of these difficult moments, one discovers the profound impact of emotional intelligence. The ability to gauge the emotional landscape of those involved, to empathize with their reactions, and to respond with sensitivity becomes paramount. It's not merely about delivering information; it's about understanding the human element—recognizing the anxiety, the disappointment, and sometimes even the anger that bad news can provoke. This awareness fosters a deeper connection with others, strengthening relationships built on trust and mutual respect.

Navigating these scenarios often illuminates the importance of clear and compassionate communication. One learns that the manner in which news is delivered can significantly influence the reception. A well-prepared project manager anticipates questions, addresses concerns proactively, and provides a transparent explanation of the circumstances. This approach not only mitigates the immediate impact but also builds a foundation of credibility and honesty that can endure beyond the crisis.

Each instance of delivering bad news also serves as a mirror, reflecting one's own emotional responses and coping mechanisms. The stress and pressure of such moments can reveal personal vulnerabilities, such as a tendency to avoid conflict or a fear of negative judgment. Acknowledging these traits is the first step towards growth, prompting introspection and the pursuit of strategies to manage them more effectively.

Moreover, these experiences underscore the value of resilience. The ability to remain composed under pressure, to recover from setbacks, and to maintain a forward-looking perspective is crucial. A project manager learns to view each challenge not as a defeat but as an opportunity for learning and improvement. This resilience is often bolstered by a support network—colleagues, mentors, and peers who provide guidance, share their own experiences, and offer encouragement.

Through the process of delivering difficult news, a project manager also hones the skill of strategic thinking. Anticipating the ripple effects of the news, planning for contingencies, and exploring alternative solutions become essential practices. This strategic mindset not only aids in managing the immediate fallout but also contributes to more effective project planning and execution in the future.

Reflection on these experiences can lead to a profound sense of personal growth. The journey of facing and delivering bad news cultivates a deeper understanding of oneself and one's capabilities. It fosters a greater appreciation for the complexities of human interaction and the nuances of effective communication. Ultimately, it shapes a more empathetic, resilient, and strategic project manager, equipped to handle the myriad challenges that come with the role.

In the quiet moments after the storm of delivering bad news, there lies an opportunity for reflection. It is in these moments that one can truly appreciate the growth that has occurred. The trials faced, the lessons learned, and the personal strengths uncovered all contribute to a more seasoned and capable project manager, ready to face future challenges with a renewed sense of confidence and insight.

Encouraging Continued Learning

A project manager's role often involves navigating difficult conversations, and one crucial aspect is fostering an environment where continuous learning is not only encouraged but thrives. This aspect is pivotal, especially when delivering bad news. By cultivating a culture of ongoing education, project managers can transform challenging situations into opportunities for growth and improvement.

In the realm of project management, the ability to convey unwelcome updates effectively is a skill that requires constant refinement. One must not only deliver the message but also facilitate an atmosphere where team members feel empowered to learn from setbacks. This begins with the project manager's own commitment to personal development. When team members observe their leader actively seeking knowledge and adapting to new methodologies, it sets a powerful example. The pursuit of knowledge becomes contagious, fostering a collective mindset geared towards improvement.

Creating a supportive learning environment involves more than just setting an example. It requires providing access to resources that enable team members to enhance their skills. This can be achieved through various means, such as workshops, training sessions, or even informal knowledge-sharing meetings. By offering these opportunities, project managers demonstrate their dedication to the team's growth, reinforcing the idea that every challenge is a stepping stone toward greater expertise.

Feedback plays a critical role in this learning process. When delivering bad news, it is essential to frame the conversation in a manner that highlights the lessons to be learned. Constructive feedback should be specific, actionable, and focused on improvement rather than blame. This approach not only helps team members understand what went wrong but also provides clear guidance on how to avoid similar issues in the future. Encouraging an open dialogue where team members feel comfortable discussing their mistakes without fear of retribution is key to fostering a culture of continuous learning.

Peer learning is another powerful tool. Encouraging team members to share their experiences and insights can lead to a richer understanding of the challenges faced and the strategies that can be employed to overcome them. This collective wisdom becomes a valuable asset, enabling the team to build on each other's strengths and mitigate weaknesses. By facilitating regular forums for knowledge exchange, project managers can harness the power of collective learning.

In addition to internal resources, looking outside the organization for inspiration and knowledge can be incredibly beneficial. Attending industry conferences, participating in webinars, or engaging with professional networks can expose the team to new ideas and best practices. This external perspective can provide fresh insights that might not be apparent within the confines of the team's immediate environment.

Ultimately, the goal is to create a resilient team that views each setback as an opportunity to learn and grow. This mindset not only enhances the team's ability to handle bad news but also prepares them to face future challenges with confidence and competence. The project manager's role is to guide this transformation, ensuring that continuous learning is embedded in the team's culture.

By fostering an environment where learning is a constant pursuit, project managers can turn the act of delivering bad news into a constructive experience. This approach not only mitigates the immediate impact of the news but also equips the team with the tools they need to improve and succeed in the long run. Through dedication to their own development and the provision of ample learning opportunities, project managers can inspire their teams to embrace a culture of continuous improvement.

Final Words of Advice

Navigating the complexities of delivering bad news as a project manager requires a delicate balance of empathy, clarity, and strategic communication. It's a task that tests not only your professional skills but also your emotional intelligence. As you stand on the threshold of these challenging conversations, there are a few key principles to keep in mind that can make the process smoother and more effective.

First and foremost, authenticity is your greatest ally. When delivering bad news, it's essential to be genuine. People can sense insincerity, and it can erode trust faster than the bad news itself. Speak from the heart, acknowledge the gravity of the situation, and show that you understand the impact it has on those receiving the news. This doesn't mean you need to be overly emotional; rather, it's about being human and recognizing the feelings of others.

Preparation is another cornerstone of effective communication in these scenarios. Anticipate the questions and concerns that might arise and prepare thoughtful responses. The more prepared you are, the more confident you will appear, and this confidence can help reassure your audience. It's also beneficial to have a clear plan for moving forward, offering solutions or next steps to mitigate the impact of the bad news.

Listening is a crucial aspect that cannot be overstated. After delivering the news, give your audience the space to process and respond. Listen actively to their concerns and feedback. This not only helps in addressing their immediate emotional reactions but also provides valuable insights that can inform your next steps. Sometimes, just being heard can significantly alleviate the distress caused by bad news.

Timing plays a pivotal role in delivering difficult messages. Choose a moment when your audience can give their full attention and when you can be fully present as well. Avoid times of high stress or when your audience is preoccupied with other pressing issues. The right timing can make a difference in how the news is received and processed.

Clarity is another essential element. Avoid jargon and ambiguous language. Be direct and to the point, but also gentle. Clear communication helps in preventing misunderstandings and allows your audience to grasp the full scope of the situation without unnecessary confusion.

Follow-up is vital after the initial delivery of bad news. Check in with your audience to address any lingering questions or concerns. This continued engagement shows that you care about their well-being and are committed to supporting them through the aftermath. It also provides an opportunity to reinforce any actions or solutions that were discussed.

Lastly, self-care is an often-overlooked aspect of delivering bad news. These conversations can be emotionally taxing, and it's important to take care of your own mental and emotional health. Seek support from colleagues or mentors, and take time to decompress and reflect on the experience. This not only helps you maintain your well-being but also prepares you to handle future challenges more effectively.

In the realm of project management, delivering bad news is an inevitable part of the role. By approaching it with authenticity, preparation, active listening, mindful timing, clarity, and dedicated follow-up, you can navigate these difficult conversations with grace and professionalism. And remember, taking care of yourself is just as important as taking care of your team.

www.ingramcontent.com/pod-product-compliance
Lightning Source LLC
Chambersburg PA
CBHW071921210526
45479CB00002B/503